Praise for Sarah Ockwell-Smith and *Ready, Set, Go!*

"I love the way Sarah breaks the concept down into clear guidelines—without being strident about one right way to be a parent—and the way she addresses the challenge of shifting from mainstream parenting to more gentle ways. The world can be a harsh place; families don't have to be."

—Lawrence J. Cohen, PhD, author of
Playful Parenting

"Provides a welcome antidote to the storm of advice that so often overwhelms new parents."

—Dr. Laura Markham, author of
Peaceful Parent, Happy Kids

"With her trademark forthright approach, Sarah Ockwell-Smith offers advice and guidance for parenting children in a way that encourages and enables them to grow and learn."

—Dr. Gill Rapley, author of *Baby Led Weaning*

"Sarah Ockwell-Smith does a fantastic job of clarifying the research, pointing out the myths we have taken as fact, and the biological realities for our little ones."

—Dr. Tracey Cassels, founder of
EvolutionaryParenting.com

"As always, Sarah has written a book that is easy to read and jam-packed with new ideas to help little ones."
    —Marneta Viegas, founder of RelaxKids.com

"Beautifully written and explains the research exceptionally well. It has just the right touch of explanation, reassurance, and science to help mothers feel confident."
    —Diana West, international board certified lactation
        consultant, La Leche League leader, and author

Ready, Set, Go!

A Gentle Parenting Guide to Calmer, Quicker Potty Training

Sarah Ockwell-Smith

A TarcherPerigee Book

tarcherperigee

An imprint of Penguin Random House LLC
375 Hudson Street
New York, New York 10014

Most TarcherPerigee books are available at special quantity discounts for bulk purchase for sales promotions, premiums, fund-raising, and educational needs. Special books or book excerpts also can be created to fit specific needs. For details, write: SpecialMarkets@penguinrandomhouse.com.

LIBRARY OF CONGRESS CATALOGING-IN-PUBLICATION DATA
Names: Ockwell-Smith, Sarah, author.
Title: Ready, set, go! : a gentle parenting guide to calmer,
quicker potty training / Sarah Ockwell-Smith.
Description: New York : Tarcher Perigee, [2017] |
Identifiers: LCCN 2018011129 (print) | LCCN 2018012002 (ebook) |
ISBN 9781524705763 (e-book) | ISBN 9780143131908 (pbk.)
Subjects: LCSH: Toilet training.
Classification: LCC HQ770.5 (ebook) | LCC HQ770.5 .O35 2017 (print) |
DDC 649/.62—dc23
LC record available at https://lccn.loc.gov/2018011129

Printed in the United States of America
1   3   5   7   9   10   8   6   4   2

Book design by Elke Sigal

Contents

CONTENTS

Introduction

There are a few milestone moments in the life of a young child that really pave the way for their future independence: sitting up, learning to crawl and walk, and eating solids are all huge achievements that signal your little one is growing up and taking charge of their own world. None of these, however, is as contentious or fraught with parental angst as when a child is learning to control their own bowel and bladder, otherwise known as potty training. No matter how you approach toileting in the first year or two of your child's life—be it with disposable diapers, cloth diapers, or diaper-free methods—there will come a time when they will transition to full control of their own toileting needs. And your role as a parent is to gently guide and lead the way, at a mindful pace, at the right time.

It sounds so simple when you think of it like that, doesn't it? But in reality, potty training is a confusing minefield spearheaded by big businesses that benefit from parental confusion and anxiety. The "helpful" information they share with parents is often full of mixed messages: to keep your child in diapers for as long as possible, with shapes and sizes to fit any age and need, versus, for example, the all-singing, all-dancing, light-up musical potty, designed to train them as soon as humanly possible. And noncommercial advice can be just as confusing. Should you praise, clap, and reward your child when they "produce," or should you approach potty training as you would any other bodily function, without fanfare? Should your child be "dry" by the time they start nursery school? Or should you potty train your baby when they are only a few months old? And what about children who start school still wearing diapers?

In recent years, parents have been increasingly shamed over potty training. If children are still in diapers when they start school, their parents are labeled negligent and lazy. If they use a potty from birth, their parents are deemed weird and "New Age." But the truth is that while the parents may act as navigators, it is the children themselves who are in the driver's seat. Your three-year-old isn't interested in whether his big brother was "dry" by his second birthday. Your daughter doesn't care that the children of your friends from baby group have all just potty trained. And your child definitely doesn't care that you are exhausted, busy, or about to start a new job when they are ready to potty train *now*.

Your role is to be informed, watchful, brave, and set to go when your child is ready—not earlier, not later. Once you've gotten started, your role is to be consistent, no matter what. Throughout this book we will look not only at your child's thoughts and feelings and "readiness" but yours too, because—as with most aspects of parenting—you're in this together, and your own emotions can have a dramatic impact on your child, positive or negative. Having worked with thousands of parents internationally in my capacity as a parenting coach, I've come to see that the gentlest, easiest, and most effective potty training happens when you work with your child, as a team. And this book provides a straightforward, evidence-based look at the process: no confusion, no mixed messages, just clear explanations and steps that work.

> You're in this together.

Potty training or toilet training?

You may have noticed that I use the term "potty training" a lot. Indeed, I have used it in the subtitle of this book. This is not to imply, however, that you *must* train your child using a potty and not a toilet. Either is fine, as we will discuss in chapter 3, and my use of the word "potty" is based solely on the fact that it translates well around the world.

Potty training or potty learning?

I am known as a strong supporter of child-led parenting—that is, allowing your child to lead and following their cues as much as possible. My view is no different when it comes to potty training. But if I believe in being child-led, then why do I focus on the word "training"? People often ask me, "If you're training them to do something, doesn't that imply you have all the control?" The *Cambridge English Dictionary* defines the word "training" as "the process of learning the skills you need to do a particular job or activity." Is it possible to be child-led and gentle, while helping children to learn the necessary skills for ditching diapers? Of course it is. Training doesn't have to mean an authoritarian approach. Sadly, I think it has become synonymous with the "baby trainers" who advocate prescriptive routines and harsh sleep interventions. However, I have trained my children to do many things while being totally empathic and compassionate to their needs. I have trained them to cross the road safely, to be careful when using sharp knives, and to stroke the cat gently rather than pull its tail. In my previous book *Gentle Discipline*, I talk about discipline being all about teaching and learning, with parents most often taking the role of a teacher and children the role of a student. But these roles can be interchangeable. And this is the case with toileting. There will be times when you are in the role of a teacher and times when you are in the role of the student, and it can be argued that whatever role you are in, training is involved as well as learning, just as it is with discipline. So I have no discomfort with the word "training," and I hope that now you don't either.

The other reason I use "potty training" as opposed to "potty learning" has, again, to do with the emotional power of vocabulary. "Potty training" is the accepted term; it is commonly used, and everyone knows what it means. It is mainstream. "Potty learning" sounds a bit alternative, and, to some, a little confusing. To illustrate my point, the term "potty training" returns 7.2 million results in an Internet search. "Potty learning" returns 1.9 million. My aim is to make gentle, mindful, evidence-based parenting mainstream. I would dearly love this book to sell as many copies as the potty-train-in-three-days-style books that take an uninformed, totally parent-led approach that is stressful for both parent and child. So, in order to reach as wide an audience as possible, I need to use the terminology with which most parents are familiar.

What is gentle potty training?

What differentiates "gentle" potty training from other styles? Ultimately, it is all about understanding—from both a scientific perspective and from that of your child. I believe that there are four main points to consider:

- **Teamwork**: gentle potty training is based on the connection between parent and child.
- **Compassion**: gentle potty training is considerate of the child's needs and feelings. There is no punishment or chastising.
- **Being informed**: gentle potty training is based on scientific knowledge and is as evidence-based as possible.
- **No rewards**: gentle potty training is achieved without chocolate candies, stickers, or heaped-on praise.

When choosing this method, it is important to be realistic. I don't promise that your child will be dry within a week, but I do promise that the whole journey will be as stress- and tear-free as possible for your whole family. Gentle potty training means more than the initial out-of-diapers-and-into-underwear goal on which so many books focus; it takes the long view and considers the potential bumps and hiccups along the way. My ultimate goal with this book is to empower both you and your child.

Using this book

Before we begin, I want to explain to you why I don't jump straight in with a list of signs of readiness. I strongly believe that the best place to start potty training is with an understanding of the body's excretory systems—that is, how pee and poo are made and excreted by the body—and how control of these systems changes from birth onward. Chapter 1, therefore, looks at exactly that. Chapter 2 looks at the research evidence behind the optimum starting age and helps you understand when the time is right for your family. Chapter 3 onward is where the action is. You may be keen to jump straight to chapter 3 in order to get started as soon as possible, but please resist the urge to skip the early chapters. It is important to start right at the beginning for the fullest understanding and, consequently, the easiest experience for both you and your child.

Ready, Set, Go!

CHAPTER 1

Physiological Readiness

In order to potty train your child as successfully and as easily as possible, it is really important that you understand the physiological functions involved. Not only can this help you select an appropriate time to commence training, it can also help you to understand and troubleshoot any problems you may face both now and in the future.

The excretory system is responsible for the elimination of waste from our bodies—primarily, urine (pee) and stools (poo). Let's take a look at how each of these works in turn.

Urinary excretion

Urine is excreted in order to eliminate the waste products of cell metabolism. It also regulates blood pressure, volume and pH, and the levels of ions such as potassium, sodium, and chloride in the body.

Urine is formed in the kidneys, a pair of small bean-shaped organs located in the upper abdomen, toward the back. Organic waste is removed by the nephron, the basic functional unit of the kidney, which filters certain objects out of the body that are not needed, while reabsorbing those that are. This process uses around 25 percent of the body's cardiac output, or blood flow. The major waste product filtered out by the kidneys is known as urea, a toxic substance formed mainly from the ammonia made by the liver during the breakdown of amino acids.

After the process of secretion and reabsorption that occurs in the nephrons, waste substances travel to the collecting tubules, where they will later be excreted in urine. Urine is mostly composed of excess water, as well as urea, excess ions, and other waste products. The amount of urine produced by the body, per kilogram of weight, reduces as we age. Newborns produce 3 ml/kg per hour, while older babies produce around 2 ml/kg and toddlers produce 1.5 ml/kg per hour. Older children produce 1 ml/kg per hour, and adults produce approximately 0.5 ml/kg per hour.[1]

The urine next passes from the kidneys through to the ureters (two tubes of smooth muscle fiber, around 30 centimeters long when fully grown) and, finally, the bladder. The bladder is a hollow, muscular, and distensible (elastic) organ that sits at the base of the pelvis. Urine leaves the bladder via the urethra, a muscular tube. Bladder capacity increases with age, until at adulthood it can hold approximately 455 ml of urine. The following table shows the capacity of the bladder at the different ages predominantly covered in this book.

Bladder capacity by age

AGE OF CHILD	BLADDER CAPACITY
SIX MONTHS	85 ML
TWELVE MONTHS	115 ML
EIGHTEEN MONTHS	142 ML
TWO YEARS	200 ML
THREE YEARS	213 ML
FOUR YEARS	227 ML
ADULT	455 ML

The process and control of urination

The neck—or section close to the opening—of the bladder is held closed by two strong bands of muscle. These are known as the internal and external sphincters. The internal sphincter is made from smooth muscle that contracts involuntarily. The external sphincter is formed of skeletal muscle and is voluntarily controlled; that is, the individual can open and close it on demand.

When the bladder is full, it signals to the parasympathetic nervous system, which, in turn, contracts a layer of the bladder composed of smooth, involuntary muscle fibers known as the detrusor muscle, causing the internal sphincter to open, ready to excrete urine. Actual urination itself is a combined response of both the parasympathetic nervous system (the part that regulates the body's unconscious actions, such as digestion) and the central nervous system, or CNS (consisting of the brain and spinal cord). This teamwork causes the internal and external sphincters to open. It is the voluntarily, CNS-controlled external sphincter that is particularly important in potty training.

It is not just the external sphincter, however, that is related to potty training but the detrusor muscle. Babies commonly urinate frequently, in small amounts. Around a third will show something known as "interrupted voiding." This is characterized by incomplete urination of varying amounts and frequency. This is due to unsustained muscular contractions of the bladder, which are, in turn, believed to be a result of poor coordination between the detrusor muscle and the sphincters of the bladder. This lack of coordination may indicate that control of the bladder in early infancy is related to connections in the developing brain rather than the detrusor muscle simply stretching and causing the internal sphincter to open, as happens later in life. This suggests that urination in babies is not completely conscious or voluntary but rather related to their brain development, like the conscious and voluntary control of their limbs and movements in the early months. This pattern disappears completely by toddlerhood when the nervous system matures.[2] Their new neurological maturity enables the toddler's and preschooler's brain to receive and send messages to the bladder, preventing urination from occurring automatically before they have found a potty or a toilet.

Control of urinary output at night

Nocturnal urinary output is controlled by the body's circadian rhythm, or body clock. At night, the lowering and, finally, absence of light is detected by the optic nerves, in the eyes, which transmit a signal to the hypothalamus and pineal gland in the brain. This signal causes several changes within the body, including:

- the secretion of melatonin—a hormone that causes sleepiness
- the lowering of body temperature
- the increased secretion of antidiuretic hormone (ADH), also known as vasopressin.[3]

Secretion of ADH causes the body to reabsorb more water and thus reduce production of urine at night. ADH is also a vasoconstrictor, which means that it constricts blood vessels within the body, leading to higher blood pressure.

This is necessary for the increased reabsorption of water at night. There is some evidence to show that in instances of persistent enuresis (bed-wetting), ADH levels are lower than in children who are dry at night; however, they are not so different that this could be considered the sole cause of bed-wetting.[4]

When thinking about babies and toddlers, it is important to understand the development of the circadian rhythm. Research shows that it develops as children grow—that is, the circadian rhythm of a baby is not comparable to that of an adult.[5] It is estimated that circadian rhythm becomes established to the level of an adult by around three years of age.[6] This maturation coincides with control of the levels of ADH production at night. Research has found that these are similar in three-year-olds and teenagers.[7] We can understand, therefore, that there is a strong correlation between the age of night dryness and the maturation of the child's circadian rhythm and ADH secretion.

Stool excretion

The intestines absorb nutrients and move any remaining waste through the body, first through the small intestine and then the large, so that it may be excreted.

The small intestine comprises the duodenum, jejunum, and ileum. In adults, it measures about twenty feet in length.

Its primary functions are to absorb nutrients from food and to break it down, ready for excretion. Small fingerlike projections, known as villi, cover the inside of the small intestine and aid in the absorption of nutrients by increasing its surface area. The small intestine adds further enzymes to those that were introduced to the food in the stomach, so continuing the process of digestion, absorption, and breaking down, as food is moved along, toward the large intestine, via a series of muscle contractions known as peristalsis.

The large intestine is about five feet in length and comprises the cecum, colon, rectum, and anal canal. The colon is a long muscular tube connecting the cecum (the first part of the large intestine) to the rectum (the last part). It is subdivided into the ascending, transverse, descending, and sigmoid colon—the ascending being connected to the cecum and the sigmoid being connected to the rectum.

As food passes through the colon, salt and water are extracted, turning soft and liquid waste into solid matter consisting of food debris and bacteria. This remains in the sigmoid colon until it is emptied into the rectum, approximately twice every day, where it is stored temporarily until stretch receptors in the rectal wall sense fullness and send a message to the brain to excrete the waste (stool or poo) via the anal canal. Like urination, the process of defecation depends on the opening of two sphincters, one internal and one external, once again a mix of involuntary and voluntary control. The internal sphincter is opened when the intrarectal pressure is increased due to the presence of waste, which pushes the internal walls of the anal canal open slightly. But as with urination, it is the external sphincter that is under our conscious control, and it is this that children must learn to master when potty training. The external sphincter is opened by the muscles of the pelvic floor, which cause the anal canal to open fully and the rectum to temporarily shorten in order to expel stools. This conscious control—or lack of it—can lead to soiling, withholding, and constipation in children. Constipation occurs when stools remain in the rectum for too long and the solid waste is moved back into the colon, where further salt and water extraction occurs. This may then lead to a buildup of hard, compacted waste. (Soiling, withholding, and constipation are discussed at length in chapter 6.)

Understanding the physiological basis of bowel and bladder control provides us with many insights into potty training. When we consider bladder capacity, detrusor muscle development, hormonal changes, and the conscious control of the external sphincters, we can appreciate that potty training, both during the day and at night, is a developmental stage, just like learning to walk and talk. It is not one that can be rushed, at least not without difficulties. Similarly, trying to delay potty training when a child is physically and psychologically ready is foolish and somewhat naive. We wouldn't try to prevent a child from walking if they had learned at a time that was inconvenient for us. Why then do so with potty training? The following chapter thus brings us naturally to the very important question: When is the right time to potty train?

CHAPTER 2

When to Begin

When should you begin potty training? I would love to give you a definitive answer, but, sadly, real life is not so black-and-white. Children do not develop at exactly the same pace; there is no internal switch that clicks "on" at some magical date. Ultimately, there is only one way to decide when it is time to begin potty training, the decision being made by one person and one person only: your child.

Does this mean that you have no involvement in the timing of potty training? Not exactly. Your role is that of watcher and waiter. You watch for certain signs and behaviors, and you wait, being mindful of your child's age. This does not mean that you are doing nothing—indeed, it could be argued that you have already begun the process of potty training by being informed and carefully observing and watching for the right time. It is an active, purposeful wait, as summed up by the late American bishop Fulton John Sheen: "Patience is power. Patience is not an absence of action; rather it is 'timing,' it waits on the right time to act, for the right principles and in the right way."

Having said that, whereas some parents do not wait long enough, some wait too long. You need to be prepared to begin as soon as your child is ready. Putting potty training off until a late age, perhaps because of certain events or inconveniences, is potentially as damaging as beginning potty training before the necessary physiological and psychological developments have taken place.

In this chapter we will look at the timing of the start of potty training, with an eye on both physiological development and the effects of emotions—yours and your child's. We will also look at some of the signs that may indicate a good time to start, as well as some that may send you in the wrong direction. Last, we will look at the potential pitfalls both of starting too early and too late.

Important physical changes to look for

As discussed in the previous chapter, there are a number of differences between adults and children when it comes to the excretory organs and their effect on continence. Let's do a quick recap of the most important points:

- **Detrusor muscle coordination:** In chapter 1 we looked at the phenomenon of incomplete voiding in babies, which is thought to be due to a lack of coordination of the detrusor muscle and communication with the brain and bladder sphincters. This incoordination disappears by the time the child enters toddlerhood.

- **Control of the external sphincters:** The act of passing pee and poo is both an involuntary and voluntary process (see page 4). The child will develop the ability to voluntarily open and close the external sphincters once the messages are sent correctly to and from the brain. This voluntary control is regulated by the child's central nervous system (CNS). The CNS develops while the child is still in utero and continues to mature after birth, as the brain makes new connections as the child grows.

- **An increase in bladder capacity:** Bladder capacity grows quickly, tripling from birth to age two, after which it slows a little. At two years of age, the bladder's capacity is 200 ml, only 27 ml smaller than it will be at age four. The full adult capacity is around 455 ml. From this perspective, therefore, any time from two years onward is a good time to begin to potty train.

- **Maturation of circadian rhythm and secretion of ADH at night:** Our body clock (circadian rhythm) controls processes in our bodies related to sleep and wakefulness. At night we secrete a hormone called ADH, which helps to reduce urination so that we may sleep uninterrupted. However, it takes until a child is around three years of age for this day/night pattern to mature. For this reason, night dryness is primarily a developmental, hormonal process that we can expect, on average, from around age three onward.

When looking at potty-training readiness from a purely physiological view, it is safe to say that we may expect a child to be dry in the daytime from two years onward and for night dryness to occur from three years onward. Of course, there will always be children who can attain voluntary dryness earlier, but this is definitely not the physiological norm. It is also possible to be "diaper-free" before this age, but it is important to understand that the dryness is superficial; while it is possible to catch pee and poo in a potty or encourage the baby to go to the potty using various conditioned cues (for instance, making certain noises), this is not true voluntary control. Does this mean that there is a problem if a child isn't out of diapers by three years of age? No, it doesn't. While the child may most likely (but not always) be physiologically able to control their body, emotionally it may be a very different story.

What science tells us about potty-training starting age

Research from Johns Hopkins University found that children under eighteen months of age have very little control over their bladder, with the average age of achieving bowel and bladder control occurring between twenty-four and thirty months.[1] This echoes findings from a longitudinal Scandinavian study that looked at bladder sensation, capacity, and postvoid residual volume (the amount of urine still in the bladder post-urination).[2] The researchers found that just more than 30 percent of two-year-olds had full bladder sensation, compared to 79 percent of three-year-olds and 100 percent of four-year-olds. Average bladder capacity doubled between one and three years. Lastly, they found that postvoid residual urine volume decreased from 5.5 ml at one year to 0 ml at three years. These results highlight an important change in bladder control between the second and third birthdays.

When it comes to bowel control, a Swiss study of more than three hundred children found that bowel control was completed in 32 percent of children at age one, 75 percent at age two, and 90 percent at age three.[3] The same study also looked at full bladder control; that is, the child was dry both during the day and at night. Researchers found that no children were dry, day and night, at age one. Between the ages of two and three, 20 percent of children were dry both day and night. By the age of five years, 90 percent were dry during the day and night.

Potty-training regressions and setbacks are common, something reflected once again in science. Research has found that 15 to 20 percent of children will continue to have wetting accidents at five years old, while further research has found that 20 percent of children under three will refuse to use the toilet or potty at any one point.[4]

What does science tell us about the repercussions of starting to potty train too early or too late? Research from Brazil has found that potty training that is started after twenty-four months is associated with a risk of persistent, or relapsing, daytime wetting.[5] The immediate question that springs to mind, however, is whether these children are struggling to maintain daytime dryness because of something other than their starting age. Is it this other variable that is delaying the achievement of reliable dryness and also pushing back the age of potty training? The Brazilian research, often quoted by those who endorse early potty training, may, in fact, be highlighting just a correlation, not a causation. There are also proven issues with later potty training, the most commonly found being that it is more likely to lead to constipation and difficulties with bowel control. Once again, however, this may be a question of correlation rather than clear causation.

Research from Philadelphia, which included 378 families, found that although early toilet training is not negatively associated with constipation, stool withholding, or toileting refusal, it does negatively affect the duration of the toilet training by prolonging it.[6] The Philadelphia study led the researchers to conclude that there are few benefits to beginning potty training before a child is twenty-seven months, at which age the duration of training is likely to be significantly shorter.

In summary, the research appears to suggest a window between twenty-four and thirty months for the easiest, most risk-free daytime potty training. Night dryness occurs somewhere between three and five years of age, although it is still normal for there to be accidents at the end of this time scale. If you are reading this book as a parent of a three- or four-year-old, however, please don't think that all is lost. Science looks at means and averages, but there are always children at the lower and upper ends of the distribution curve. Some will train much earlier and some much later. A gentle approach to potty training is based on the understanding that while there might be scientific norms, children are all individuals.

Why potty training takes place later now than fifty years ago

One question I'm asked again and again is "Why are children today potty training so late?" It is true that today's generation stays in diapers considerably longer than we did, and we, in turn, remained in diapers a lot longer than our parents. In many other cultures children are diaper-free from the very early months, if not from birth. Does this mean that we are delaying training our children because of laziness? Or have we fallen prey to advertising and sponsorship from the disposable-diaper industry?

While there is no doubt that disposable diapers may initially be perceived to be easier to use than reusables, the cloth-diaper industry is once again growing and ever improving, and those who have tried them know that they require far less labor than the terry cloth squares secured with safety pins of earlier generations. Disposables are no longer the life-changing innovation they once were, although they are definitely cheaper than they were fifty or so years ago, which means more can afford them.

While I don't think that parents today are so selfish as to leave their children in environmentally damaging diapers long past the age of bladder and bowel control capability in order to make their own lives easier, there is no denying that families are busier and far more mothers are working, and that this may, therefore, play a role. Nevertheless, I believe the biggest reason for the potty-training age being later than it used to be is *knowledge*. The increase in scientific understanding over the last twenty-five years helps us to make an informed choice about starting age; one that is based upon the true physiological and psychological capabilities of our children. Alongside this, we are, fortunately, moving away from the behaviorist and authoritarian parenting that was so common in the last century. Our approach to potty training today is not only more informed but more mindful and more child-led and, consequently, more in line with the true age of readiness.

Signs of readiness

Pick up almost any book or leaflet on potty training and you will find an entry titled "Signs of Readiness." I have, therefore, included this section here because I suspect readers are expecting to see it. After all, how do you know when to start potty training? Surely you need a sign?

In fact, the idea of waiting for signs of readiness is something of a misconception. If we viewed potty-training readiness in terms of certain tick-box moments, most would be invisible. For instance, it is not possible for parents to ascertain when their child's bladder capacity has reached 200 ml or 227 ml, if their central nervous system is mature enough to have complete control over the external sphincters, or if their circadian rhythm is mature. It is technically possible, therefore, that a child may be physiologically ready to potty train but show no obvious outward behavioral signs.

Conversely, many true behavioral signs of readiness are actually quite subtle and are, as such, often overlooked. I think sometimes parents are waiting for a huge green-light moment, with streamers and fanfare. Reality is rarely like that. In most cases, the parent chooses when to begin, making a decision that takes into account physiology based upon age, some quiet cues from the child, and their own instinct.

Confusingly, there are also many behaviors that are commonly believed to indicate potty-training readiness but really aren't. So let's look at some of the myths and true signs, subtle or otherwise, that can be useful indicators.

Potty-training readiness myths

Many of what parents take as signs that their child is ready are actually just normal childhood behaviors with no direct link to potty training. These include:

- Telling you that they have done a pee or poo after they have done it (especially if they are not bothered by it) or while they are doing it; potty training is all about a child knowing that they need to go *before* they have done anything, so while awareness is a good start, this type of statement needs to be before the act, not during or after.

- Taking off their diaper (simply great fun for many children).

- Playing with poo taken from a soiled diaper (an excellent renewable source of finger paint and clay that they have produced themselves).

- Following you to the toilet (if your little one has separation anxiety, you will know this happens from an early age).

- Hating diaper changes (this is universal among all children, I think).

Signs to watch for

While there are doubtless many signs that are strong indicators of potty-training readiness, don't be fooled into believing that your child must show them before beginning. Some children are ready to potty train yet don't give their parents any pointers. (I have trained two children quite smoothly who showed me no signs whatsoever that they were ready to begin, and I'm not sure if they ever would have indicated readiness in any way had I just waited it out.)

The following could suggest that starting to potty train imminently is a good idea:

- They hide to poo or are reluctant to poo in your presence or the presence of others.

- They are able to dress and undress with minimal assistance from you. In particular, they are able to pull trousers and underwear up and down.

- They are able to communicate verbally with you about simple body sensations (for instance, "I'm hot" or "I'm hungry").

- They sometimes tell you that they need to go to the toilet before they actually go.

- They can follow a chain of two or three simple instructions—for instance, "Go to the cupboard, get your shoes. Now put your shoes on."

- They sometimes ask to have their diaper changed, or they bring you a new diaper without being prompted.

- They are mostly dry when they wake from a nap (for night training they should be mostly dry when they wake in the morning).

- Their diaper remains dry for a period of two hours or more at a time (this can indicate increasing bladder capacity).

If you can match one or two signs from this list along with an appropriate potty-training age, then you have a very high chance of straightforward and successful potty training.

Girls before boys?

Another myth is that girls are ready to potty train before boys. There is no truth to this, despite the number of people who believe in it. There is no difference in the speed of physiological maturation of the bladder or bowel and no behavioral reasons why girls should be easier and faster to train than boys. Yet it seems, sadly, that we have created a bit of a self-fulfilling prophecy: If parents believe boys are harder to train, they are more likely to start later with them and enter into the training period with a negative mind-set. Later training and lowered expectations could very well lead to problems that do not have a biological cause and could have been avoided. As long as your child is of an appropriate age and, ideally, showing a sign or two of readiness, it makes no difference if they are male or female.

What comes first—pee or poo?
Day or night?

Although bowel control develops slightly earlier than bladder control, daytime training of both tends to occur together. You may find it easier to spot signs of an approaching poo than a pee, and the longer time taken to poo does also give you an opportunity to redirect your child quickly to the potty or toilet. For this reason, you may initially find poos easier than pees when you start potty training. This isn't always the case, though, and it is common for children to initially struggle with poos out of diapers (an issue covered in chapter 6).

What about bowel control at night versus during the day? Daytime almost always occurs first. Usually, you would expect a child to be dry in the daytime for at least six months to a year before the same can be said of nights. Often it takes a lot longer. Chapter 5 specifically considers nighttime training.

When not to start potty training

I personally believe that as many people delay potty training for too long as those who start too early. Neither is child-led, and both can present problems. Ultimately, there is only one "wrong" time to start potty training—when your child is not physiologically or emotionally ready. If their body and brain have matured to a certain level, then technically there are no times to avoid starting to potty train. However, the reality of parenting is that it isn't always convenient. Just like buses, new developmental achievements all seem to come along at once. Usually they will also come at a time when you have just started a new job, are moving house, or are about to welcome another baby to the family. It may be tempting to put off potty training until things calm down, but then often something else will crop up and then something else and, before you know it, several months have passed.

All that being said, potty training does require as much of your focus and attention as possible, at least in the first couple of weeks. For this reason, there are a handful of times when I would try to temporarily delay the start of potty training. These are:

- If a new baby has just arrived (and by just arrived, I mean a week or two ago) or is expected imminently (i.e., you are thirty-eight-weeks-plus pregnant).

- If your child is ill—wait until they are back to full strength, even if it's just a minor cold or they are under the weather or in pain for some reason.

- If your child has just experienced a major change in their life (for instance, starting nursery, moving house, or parents separating) and they haven't yet adjusted to it well.

In addition, there are four other very specific reasons *not* to start potty training. If you find yourself in any of these situations, please resist the urge to buckle under the pressure. It will most likely not end well:

- **Your childcare provider has told you that your child should be out of diapers before they start, or that they**

will not change your child's diaper. Aside from this not being a good reason to potty train, the organization or individual is on very shaky ground: Technically, they are discriminating against your child and their needs.

- **Your older child was out of diapers by now.** Every child is an individual. They don't all meet the same physical development milestones at the same time. There is no specific date at which children are physiologically ready for potty training or when they are emotionally ready. There was a range of several months between my own children. My youngest was just under two years old, and my oldest was almost three. There was an even bigger variation in nighttime dryness achievement.

- **It is summer.** While it may be wonderful to potty train in the garden with a naked child, narrowing down the months of the year when it can take place to two or three is a recipe for disaster. I have come across so many parents who have tried to potty train too soon in order to try to get it out of the way in the summer and a similar number who have put it off for far too long, waiting for the colder, indoor months to pass. Watch your child, not your calendar.

> Watch your child, not your calendar.

- **All of your friends' children of the same age are out of diapers.** There is no fun in being the only parent in a group whose child is still in diapers. Most of this anxiety and pressure, however, comes from yourself. There is no race to dryness, nor are there medals to be won. Nobody will be interested in the age your child was out of diapers once they're in school; in fact, there is a strong likelihood you won't even remember yourself. Parental guilt, anxiety and competition are perhaps the worst reasons to begin—and the best reasons to pause and redirect your attention to your child's readiness and needs.[7]

To conclude, there is no perfect starting time. Well, aside from the time when your child is ready, that is.

No matter the season, the inconvenience, or your personal feelings, the only time to train is when your child is physiologically and psychologically mature enough. Don't wait until you feel less tired or busy, or for the nice weather that's been forecast for two weeks' time, or until your newborn has turned three months old. And don't try to potty train before your new baby is born, before you move house, or before you return to work. I cannot stress this enough—put your feelings and convenience aside as much as you can. Ironically, you will find that your own well-being will benefit.

27

What if my three-and-a-half-year-old is not yet potty trained?

While I can't deny that I have written this book predominantly for those who are new to potty training and thinking of starting, it is also for those who have already had false starts. If you have previously tried potty training with little success, or you are struggling with certain issues, I hope you will find something in each chapter that will help. Chapter 6 in particular is all about what to do when things aren't going, or haven't gone, to plan.

As I've said, starting to potty train at a time that is right for your child is one of the biggest keys to success. So too is getting ready to start. By which I mean preparation, preparation, preparation: Prepare yourself with knowledge, prepare your child emotionally, and prepare practically with the right equipment. Chapter 3 is all about the preparation.

CHAPTER 3

Getting Ready to Start

You've decided the time is right to begin potty training. Or perhaps you have decided that you would like to plan a little in advance—something I definitely recommend. What do you need in order to be "ready to go"? This chapter looks at some of the practical and emotional preparation you can do before you actually begin potty training your child.

Let's start with the practical side of things.

Potty or toilet trainer seat and/or toilet?

I am often asked, "Is it better to use a potty or go straight for the big toilet?" I don't think there is a definitive answer, aside from "Whatever your child prefers." There are pros and cons for doing it either way, though the potty is often the better option.

Using a potty is more portable, allowing you to potty train in any room of the house. If you have a house with only an upstairs toilet, I would certainly recommend starting with a potty. Trying to run up the stairs with a desperate toddler isn't fun. The same is true if you live in an old house with the bathroom downstairs, particularly when it comes to middle-of-the-night toilet runs. If you are lucky enough to live in a house with both an upstairs and a downstairs toilet, or if you live in a ranch or apartment, then you may choose to use the toilet from the start.

Potties can seem less intimidating to children than "the big toilet," as they are sized to them. Their portability can also help when it comes to poo time—many children like to hide when having a poo, and potties allow for this without being shut in another room with the door closed. Another advantage is that no special steps or seats are required when using a potty, which ultimately means they are less expensive too.

The downside of using a potty is that your child will have to transition to the big toilet at some point. In most cases this transition is smooth, but in others less so.

Using the big toilet

The major positive in using the big toilet from the start is that children can see you using it and understand what it is for. Initially, a potty may be a strange concept to them, and it is not something that you can model. Despite this, I'd still recommend starting with a potty. This gives you more flexibility than using a toilet, predominantly because it is portable, meaning your child doesn't have to move long distances in the first few days of training, which can help to prevent accidents.

Choosing a potty

Potty shopping can be confusing. There is an overwhelming range of choices. Should you get one that plays a tune, one that lights up, one that has a spout for easier emptying, one that has wheels, one that has arms, one that has a chair back, or one that holds a tablet for the child to watch videos while they are sitting on it? (The answer to the latter is definitely not, by the way!)

I don't believe that you need to buy an all-singing, all-dancing potty. Basic will suffice. In fact, basic is almost always better, as it doesn't take away from the process of learning. If children realize that they can make a potty light up or play a tune when they pee into it, they can quickly be incentivized to use it for the wrong reason. The only right reason to use a potty is when they need to go to the toilet—anything else has the power to teach them to override their body's sensations and needs.

I have only four must-haves when looking for the perfect potty:

1. The potty must be a good fit for the child. Different ones suit different body types. Make sure that the seat is not too narrow or too wide for your child. They should be able to sit on it comfortably without looking squashed or like the seat isn't able to support them.

2. The potty should be positioned so that the child can sit in it with their feet flat on the floor. Ideally, they should be in a slight squat position, with their bottom a little lower than their knees.

3. The potty should support their lower back, just enough that they do not end up leaning backward, wobbling, or struggling to find their center of gravity.

4. The potty should sit steadily on the floor. Watch to see if it might tip up easily or skid out from underneath the child.

If the potty is in your child's favorite color or decorated with their favorite character, so much the better, but this isn't necessary. The chances are, if you've picked the right time to start, your child will be excited enough about learning to use the potty and getting out of diapers without needing any added incentives.

Choosing a toilet trainer seat and step

If you opt to start on the big toilet, or you want to plan ahead for its use, you will need a good toilet trainer seat and step. As with potties, your main aim is to find a seat that is a good fit for your child. The seat should sit snugly on the toilet and shouldn't slip around. Seats that are a poor fit can be scary to children and can really put them off using a regular toilet.

I would avoid padded toilet trainer seats, if possible. These may look more comfortable and thus appealing, but they can delay the transition from potty to toilet seat and toilet seat to main toilet. If your child is used to sitting on a potty with a hard seat, the padded trainer seat can be confusing for them, and if they are used to using a padded trainer seat, they may not be keen on a hard toilet seat in the future.

A good step is a vital accompaniment to a toilet trainer seat. It is important that your child is never sitting on the toilet seat with their legs dangling in the air. Their feet should always be flat on a solid surface, whether that is the floor or a step. As well as helping them to poo (as discussed in chapter 6), it can help them to feel safer and more supported. Once again, make sure the step is substantial enough to not slip around. Ideally, it will have rubber along the bottom edges to keep it in position. It is possible to buy toilet trainer seats and steps in one; these look a little like a ladder with handrails at the side of the seat and are probably the ultimate in helping a child to feel safe and stable, but they're not always necessary if you get a well-fitting separate seat and step.

When should you introduce a potty to the house?

Many parents introduce a potty into their home, especially their bathroom, months before potty training begins. The theory behind this is that the presence of the potty becomes accepted, and children get used to it and are happy to be around it. This is said to reduce fear and anxiety when potty training begins. I agree with this to a degree, but I believe that many bring potties into the home far too early. If you do it several months before potty training begins, the purpose of the potty is lost. It becomes just another object around the house and, most important, one that isn't specifically used for going to the toilet.

I do recommend introducing a potty before you begin training but ideally one to two weeks in advance, and certainly no more than a month. This is enough time for the child to get used to the potty and practice sitting on it, but not so much that they lose interest and no longer associate it with actually going to the toilet. Children of potty-training age struggle with abstract and hypothetical thought. They live very much in the here and now, and their brains are not developed enough to think long into the future or about what-ifs. So while you may be able to picture them sitting on a potty and having a pee or a poo in six months' time, this isn't something that they are able to do. The arrival of a potty should signal potty training that is imminent, but not so imminent that the child is given no time at all to get used to it.

Underwear or pull-ups?

Pull-ups (disposable diapers with elasticated waists that can be pulled up and down like regular underwear) may seem like a great product to use when potty training. They can give the child the feel of wearing underwear, while being able to contain any accidents. What's not to like? Actually, a lot. Pull-ups give a mixed message: "I think you are ready to potty train but I don't trust you, so here's a diaper for when you make mistakes." Once you begin to potty train your child, it is really important that your message is clear and confident: "I think you are ready to potty train, and I trust that you don't need a diaper anymore" (at least in the daytime). Pull-ups have no place in potty training. The only times that they can be useful are, first, if you are not yet potty training and your child hates to lay down for diaper changes and, second, if your child is older and not

> **Pull-ups have no place in potty training.**

yet nighttime trained or is still bed-wetting regularly, in which case they can seem less diaperlike and therefore less likely to upset them when they are used at night.

Once you decide it is time to potty train, you need to lose the diapers during the day. Underwear or bare-bottomed is the way to go (there is a place for both, as we will discover in the next chapter).

What do you look for in good underwear? Anything that is comfortable. Find a brand and a cut that is appropriate for your child's build. As with almost all children's clothing, stereotyping abounds. Boys' underwear tends to be roomier and more generously cut than girls', which, even from a very young age, verges on skimpy and is more about aesthetics than practicality. Boys' underwear, therefore, can often be more comfortable than girls', whoever is wearing it. Find some in your child's favorite color and design and, most important, go shopping for it together. Buying underwear is a big deal. Talk to your child in advance about your special shopping trip and how exciting it will be. Ask their opinion and trust it as much as possible, even when your little boy wants to buy flowery unicorn knickers or your daughter wants to buy Spider-Man underpants. If your child is happy with their underwear, they will be more likely to want to ditch diapers.

As with introducing a potty, purchasing underwear should happen a week or two ahead of training but ideally no more, due to children's lack of abstract and hypothetical thought.

Potty-friendly clothing

Giving some thought to your child's potty-training wardrobe is another important part of your preparation. Clothes that are too restrictive and difficult for the child to manage by themselves can cause wetting and soiling accidents, which may dent your child's confidence and delay continence.

Let's start with what children *shouldn't* wear when potty training:

- Trousers or shorts with zips, hooks, or button closures at the waist
- Tight-fitting skirts that are hard to pull up without adult help
- Tights
- Leggings
- Bodysuits with snaps at the crotch
- Tops with dangly ties
- Denim jeans
- Long or flowing dresses
- Belts

This doesn't mean that your child can never wear anything on this list again, simply that you should wait until potty training is well established. At the beginning you really want to avoid clothing that can hamper their progress.

Many people choose to keep their children naked when

they potty train, which works really well in the summer months but less so in the winter in colder climates, for obvious reasons. A short-term compromise is to keep the child bare-bottomed; that is, wearing a top only. This can work well for the first day or two of potty training but is not something I recommend for too long. Children who potty train bare-bottomed for a prolonged period of time can often struggle with continence when they are fully clothed, especially when they are out of the house and in day care. The ideal is to potty train your child as quickly as possible fully clothed, but with clothes that are potty-training friendly. My ideal wardrobe for potty training includes:

- Baggy trousers and shorts with elasticated waists; the child should be able to pull them up and down quickly and easily without adult help (tracksuit bottoms are ideal).
- Tops that finish above waist-length and are fairly fitted (regular T-shirts, for example).
- Short, A-line jersey T-shirt dresses (big, twirly skirts aren't good).
- Baby leg warmers (these work well in colder months to help keep little legs warm on the first few days of training).

Your child's potty-training clothes should ideally not be newly purchased for the occasion. There are two reasons for this: First, a whole new wardrobe can be unsettling for children, as is potty training, and you don't want too much change at once; second, their clothes are likely to get covered in pee and poo and will need to be frequently washed.

Potty-proofing your home

Potty training can get messy. I have never heard of a child who hasn't had an accident while training. You will get pee or poo (or both) on your floor and your child's clothes, and they will wet the bed when you progress to nighttime toilet training. Again, preparation can save you a lot of stress further down the line.

Before you begin, think about ways in which to minimize damage to your home and the items in it. If you have wooden floors in your living area, you will need to invest in lots of towels, cloths, and floor cleaner. You may also want to buy a waterproof sheet or plastic dropcloth to keep moisture out of them (shower curtains work well too). If you have carpets in your living area, you are going to need to think about waterproofing, and the same goes for beds when you progress to nighttime potty training. If you have a beloved area rug in your living room, it might be a good idea to roll it up and temporarily store it elsewhere as a precaution. You may also want to use a fleece blanket or throw over any sofas or chairs on which your child ordinarily sits, just in case.

These are my suggested products for potty-proofing your home:

- A stack of old towels and cloths (for mopping up and cleaning accidents)
- Carpet spot cleaner
- Hard-floor cleaner
- A good mattress protector or bed mats (the larger ones intended for use with elderly incontinence are not only better, but cheaper)
- A waterproof sheet, old shower curtain, or large piece of PVC-coated tablecloth
- Some form of air freshener or natural oils in a diffuser (my preference)

Potty-training hygiene

If you haven't already had conversations with your child about hygiene, now is a great time to start. You need to be careful to make these conversations balanced. It is important your child understands and adopts appropriate personal hygiene, but you don't want to go too far and make them scared of germs or obsessive about cleanliness.

When it comes to hand washing, a good way to approach the subject is to talk about "good" and "unwanted" germs. Explain that germs are tiny creatures, so small that we cannot see or feel them. Some of them are our friends—they help to keep us healthy, and we call them "good bacteria" or "good germs." Others, however, don't help us and can even make us sick—we call these "unwanted bacteria" or "unwanted germs." Explain that in order to keep the good germs and get rid of the unwanted ones, we need to wash our hands when we have been to the toilet. Young children aren't known for their hand-washing skills, and often this is something you also have to teach. Of course, the very best way to teach hand washing is to demonstrate it for your child. You could suggest to them that they need to count slowly while washing their hands and that they shouldn't stop before they get to ten. Or a more fun way, perhaps just the first time you are teaching them, is to mix some glitter in a saucer with a small amount of glue and water and then get your child to put the mix all over their hands. Tell them to imagine the glitter is unwanted germs that need to be washed off. Go with them to the sink and encourage them to wash their hands until the last bit of glitter is gone. Explain that although the unwanted germs on their hands are invisible (unlike the glitter), they should imagine that they are washing them off (like the glitter).

Although I am a fan of teaching good hand washing as soon as possible, I am most definitely *not* in favor of antibacterial hand wash, soaps, sprays, and wipes. We seem to have an increasing obsession with these products, yet they are no more effective than ordinary soap and water and may even bring their own health risks. For instance, much of the safety data on the common ingredient known as triclosan comes from animal studies. This means that we really don't have much of an idea of how safe it is to use on a regular basis. The US Food and Drug Administration has declared that after forty years of study, they have found no evidence to suggest that household products containing antibacterial ingredients are more effective than soap and water.[1]

A good hand-washing station will therefore consist of nothing more than a sink, a step, some soap, and a towel. Liquid soap, from a hand-pump dispenser, means you don't have to worry about bars of soap slipping out of little hands, but some can be quite stiff to use, so check the pumping action for child-friendliness. Keep a towel within reach for hand drying and, most important, a step next to the sink so that your child can reach everything without adult assistance.

Alongside hand washing, you also need to think about wiping. The big question here is: wipes or toilet paper? Until this point, you and your child have probably both gotten used to wipes (whether disposable or reusable), but although they will still play a role in potty training, they will have less of a place than before. Unless your child has a big accident of the poo variety, now is the time to introduce them to toilet paper. Explain to them what it is for and how much to use, and let them see you using it, telling them that soon they will be using it too, when it is time for potty training. Toilet paper is something worth paying more for when it comes to potty training. Scratchy, hard paper can, understandably, be very off-putting to young children, so it's important to choose something soft.

Equipment for outside the home

In chapter 4 we will look at potty training in the home, when to go out, and how to manage when you're away from home. Once again, preparation is key. Purchasing and preparing a few basics can turn what could be a potentially stressful event into one that you can take in stride.

These are my must-haves:

- A piddle pad—a protective pad to use in the car seat and stroller (one that is slightly padded and can be machine washed is best) is a great asset.

- A wet bag—a bag with a waterproof liner for transporting wet and soiled clothes; a string bag, lined in a plastic fabric, is good (these are sold by real/cloth diaper retailers).

- A travel potty—you can simply take your regular potty out with you in a waterproof bag or you can buy one that folds up, specifically designed for travel. You won't need to use this for long, but it does help if you need to go out of the house before your child is fully confident using an adult toilet.

- A prepacked bag containing at least two clean items of underwear, two clean pairs of trousers or shorts, a spare top, and a pair of clean socks. Keep this in the bottom of your stroller or in the trunk of your car so that it is always with you if you leave the house—there is nothing worse than realizing your child has had an accident and you have no clean, dry clothing to change them into.

- A toilet roll and a packet of wipes—never rely on public toilets being well stocked with toilet paper, and the wipes will be a godsend for any accidents, as well as for cleaning up the potty after use.

This may seem like an awful lot of equipment to take out with you, and it is. You won't be doing this forever, though. Once your child is reliably dry, you can drop right down to just a packet of wipes and some toilet paper and perhaps a spare pair of trousers and underwear.

Preparation for parents who work full time

I am well aware that many reading this book will now be thinking, *This sounds like a lot of work. How am I ever going to fit this in while I'm working?* Potty training does require some time and thought, but it is mostly in the preparation, rather than the execution. This preparation can fit around your regular workweek, and here the Internet is your friend for shopping. However, when it comes to actually beginning potty training, you do need to consider the time you have available to devote to it.

My recommendation is that you allow a block of three days in a row as a minimum, but ideally seven. This doesn't mean that by the end of three (or even seven) days your child will be totally potty trained. This is unlikely to happen. However, the first few days are the most important, so try to devote as much time to it at this stage as you can. If you are unable to take time off work, then at the very least start on a Saturday morning that, ideally, starts a three-day weekend, so that you are also at home on the Monday. Perhaps you are off over a holiday break? Or perhaps you have some extra vacation days you can use? Basically, the more time you can take off work, the better. I have worked with parents who have managed with only a weekend, but it is important to understand that these are the minority.

Can potty training be split between two parents or other family members?

Continuity is key in the first few days, so this isn't ideal, but as long as the other adult is fully on board with the methodology and has been included in the preparation, and the child has a strong attachment and a good relationship with them, the chances are it will go well.

Can potty training be split between parents and day care?

Here, I am more reluctant. While there are usually not too many issues with day care after three or four days of potty training at home, the bulk of the potty training in the first few days should happen in one location. If this is really not possible, you must be on the same page as your day-care provider. They must understand your approach (and ideally read this book), and the lines taken at home and in day care must be identical. Training at day care should also be under-taken by one member of staff only—ideally, the one who has the strongest relationship with your child. Ultimately, the more you can do yourself, the better.

Preparing your child's diet

One of the biggest stumbling blocks when it comes to potty training is constipation (this is discussed at some length in chapter 6). Avoiding this in the first place is obviously so much easier than dealing with it once it's happened. Focusing on healthy levels of hydration and fiber in your child's diet now can pay dividends in the long run.

Fluids

Children should be encouraged to drink plenty of fluids, but not before a meal. (Drinking lots before a meal can reduce appetite, which means less fiber will be consumed.) You will hear many people say that we should drink six to eight glasses of water per day. This is not strictly true, however, and while this is in the ballpark of what most people should drink, the best indicator is urine color. In a healthy, well-hydrated body, urine will be a very pale straw color. If your child's urine is yellowy or even orange, then they are dehydrated and need to drink more.

Fiber

How much fiber should your child eat, and where should it come from? By the age of three, the average child in Western society eats around 11 grams of fiber per day. The recommended amount at this age, however, is a minimum of 19 grams per day. This shortfall is worrying and problematic, especially when it comes to potty training, because fiber helps food to move along the digestive tract by acting as a bulking agent and absorbing water, so a lack of it can cause slowed digestion and difficulty passing poo, which can cause long-term continence issues.

The following foods are all good sources of fiber:

- Whole grains—from cereal and bread
- Berries
- Oranges
- Bananas
- Pears (with skin)
- Peas

- Beans
- Sweet potatoes
- Regular potatoes, baked and eaten in their skins
- Apples (with skin)
- Lentils
- Sweet corn
- Brown rice

If your child is picky about fruit and vegetables (as most children of potty-training age are), think of ways to make them more appealing:

- Dried fruit, coated in yogurt or chopped up and added to breakfast cereal
- Stewed fruit used in a crumble, or mixed into yogurt
- Smoothies made with fruit and vegetables (vegetables are quite hard to detect in smoothies)
- Fruit breads and cakes made with real fruit—for instance, banana bread or carrot cake
- Grated vegetables and/or lentils in pasta sauces
- Vegetable sticks (carrot, cucumber, pepper, etc.) with a favorite dip for a snack

Working on the level of fiber in your child's diet before potty training is one of the most important preparations that you can make, so starting early is a good idea.

Preparing your child emotionally

Preparing your child physically goes hand in hand with preparing them emotionally. Potty training will be most successful when the child is ready both in body and in mind. Yet this aspect is glossed over by far too many parents. So although you may be itching to get started, don't skip this preparation. It really matters.

How do you prepare your child emotionally? There are four main stages. Let's look at each of them in turn.

1. **Share your knowledge with your child.** Demystifying helps to remove any fear your child may have around the processes involved and the purpose of going to the toilet, as well as making them more interested in their bodily functions. Spend some time talking about what pee and poo are, how they are made, and why it is important that they don't stay inside us. A good children's book is important here, with pictures and simple explanations of the biology, not just one that is focused on actually using a potty (see pages 177–8 for recommendations). The Internet is also very handy—search for videos specifically for children and simple illustrations.

2. **Normalize toileting.** If you have previously been a "closed-door" family (i.e., going to the bathroom on your own), now is the time to drop the privacy and pee and poo with the door open. When you go to the toilet, talk about what you are doing—"Can you hear the pee coming out into the toilet?" or "Did you hear the plop when my poo came out?" Invite your child to look at your poo in the toilet bowl (especially if you have eaten corn recently!) or pass you some toilet paper. This may all be incredibly alien and awkward at first, but your ease (or not) around talking about toileting will spread to your child. If you are hung up about it, they will be too. In some ways this step is also to help parents; when you become more relaxed and open, you will find potty training so much easier.

3. **Teach the words for genitals.** If you haven't already had a discussion with your child about the anatomically correct name for their genitals, now is the time. Knowing the correct words (penis for boys and vulva or vagina for girls—vulva is technically correct, because it is actually the interior tube that is called the vagina) is important—not only for potty training but also to help remove any embarrassment surrounding their own bodies. It's fine if your child chooses to call their penis or vulva something else, so long as they know the correct terms and are happy to use them as well.

4. Urine, tinkle, number one, pee, or something
else? As well as knowing the correct names for their
body parts, children should also know the words for
urine and stools for much the same reason. When
you talk about either, it is important to use commonly accepted names. For this book I have chosen
to use pee and poo, as this is what most people call
them and I don't want it to sound too much like a
medical textbook. This is very important for when
your child is at day care or visiting friends. You may
know that "a tinkle" means that your child needs a
pee, but not everybody else will. Using the most
common everyday terminology will ultimately be
most helpful.

Removing any embarrassment around toileting and
helping children to name and understand their own bodily
functions can encourage them to take ownership of some of
their potty training. A motivated and relaxed child is one
who will take to the process more easily.

By choosing the physiologically appropriate age for your
child and putting some preparation into place before beginning, you dramatically increase the chances of potty
training being as calm and straightforward as possible. It isn't

always easy or achieved in three days (as some books unrealistically claim), but with knowledge, some groundwork, and a plan, it can be a stress-free and even enjoyable experience for the whole family.

Ready? Let's go!

CHAPTER 4

Let's Go!

Along with weaning onto solids and encouraging our child to walk into our open arms for the first time, I think potty training is one of the most exciting stages we go through with them. By putting in place the preparations described in the previous chapters, alongside the approach I'll describe in this one, you will be able to embrace potty training with excitement, not trepidation.

Confidence

One aspect that many potty-training books don't talk about is how you, the parent, feel. Your feelings really do matter, though, and are one of the keys to successful potty training.

If I had to single out the most important feeling for parents at this stage, it would surely be confidence: confidence in your decision to begin potty training and confidence in your child's ability. If you are not confident at this point, it is important to ask why. Having read chapters 1 to 3, do you doubt your child's physiological or psychological readiness? If you instinctively feel that now is not the right time for your child, then perhaps you would be better off revisiting this chapter in a month or two. If you doubt *yourself,* read on.

Children are often ready to potty train before their parents are ready to potty train them. Perhaps you are a little sad that your baby is growing up? Perhaps you are feeling exhausted emotionally or physically and would prefer to delay until you feel better? Unfortunately, I don't think these are reasons to delay, nor are they reasons to question your child's abilities. But how do you get around this?

Start by rereading the section on signs of readiness in chapter 2, to reassure yourself that this *is* the right time. Trust in your child and, perhaps most important, trust in yourself; chances are you are a far better, more competent parent than you think you are. Then work through the steps in this chapter, one by one. If any doubts creep in, remind yourself that you and your child can do it—together.

> Remind yourself that you and your child can do it—together.

Practicalities

In the previous chapter we looked at some of the general considerations of potty training; now let's take a look at what your potty-training setup will look like in more detail. What should your home look like for the first few days and weeks of potty training? In which room should you place the potty? When should you introduce underwear and clothing? And for parents of little boys, should they sit or stand?

Pick your location

Do you know which room you want to potty train in? For many, their thoughts turn immediately to their bathroom or, if they have one, a downstairs toilet. This makes sense. After all, this is where you go to the toilet, and by now your child should be used to seeing you go. And from a hygiene perspective, you may want to keep the potty in your bathroom or toilet too, as the floors are likely the easiest in your home to clean. Despite good arguments for the bathroom or toilet, however, the best place to potty train initially is actually your main living area. For the first few days, at least, you, your child, and the potty need to be in the same room as much as possible. You may get very little warning of an imminent pee or poo and running to another room may take longer than your child can manage.

If you do move to a different room for any length of time

(longer than half an hour), take the potty with you. For instance, if you are making dinner in the kitchen, move the potty into the kitchen area. If you are in the bathroom, for bath and bedtime, take the potty into the bathroom with you. But otherwise, try to stay in your living room with the potty.

On the first day of potty training, ask your child where in the living room they would like to keep their potty. When the exact location is decided, prepare the area by putting down the waterproof sheets or shower curtains you have bought (see page 40).

What about going out?

You'll need to stay in your home for the first two days as an absolute minimum. Then, depending on how your child is getting on, you can consider going out on day three, although most children will do better staying in for a third day. When you do go out, it is important that you take a potty with you. We will look at what to do when you are away from home in more detail at the end of this chapter (see page 73).

Dressing your child

In the previous chapter we looked at potty-friendly clothing (see page 38). On day one, and ideally day two as well, you should keep your child naked from the waist down. If you are potty training in winter and your house is cold, then the baby leg warmers I mentioned on page 38, along with some socks, can help to keep their legs and feet warm. Starting off totally bare-bottomed for the first day or two is really important. You are likely to get very little warning that your child needs to go to the toilet, and trying to take off trousers or pull down underwear can take just that little bit too long, meaning that accidents are more likely to happen. Similarly, a complete absence of underwear and trousers means that your child will be more aware of the sensations of pee or poo (as they are doing them). For this reason, it is imperative that you avoid diapers in the daytime the minute you start to potty train your child. Whatever the style of diaper, they must go and you must try as hard as you can to resist putting them back on in the daytime, especially if you leave the house. This is why staying at home is important for the first couple of days.

On day three (or two if your child copes really well on day one) it is time to introduce underwear. You may be tempted to delay this for a few more days, until accidents have stopped. While this may seem like a good idea, especially from the point of view of laundry, keeping underwear off for more than three days can lead to problems with potty training. If a child strongly associates using the potty with being bare-bottomed, they may struggle with the concept while wearing underwear. Introducing it by day three should prevent this.

If you need to leave the house on day three or four, then dress your child in clothing that is easy for them to pull up and down—so no tights, buttons, or buckles yet. A simple pair of elasticated tracksuit bottoms or a short skirt and bare legs are best (perhaps with some leg warmers on colder days). If you can stay at home for a couple of days, try to manage without full clothing until day five. Even then, stick to clothing that's easy to pull up and down. Your child should be able to undress themselves enough to go to the toilet easily without you and shouldn't need help pulling their underwear and clothing back up. Stick with these potty-training-friendly clothes until your child is reliably trained. For some, this may be by the end of the first week; for others, it may take a month or more, but only at this point should you return to clothing that takes them longer to put on and take off.

Standing versus sitting

One of the questions I am asked most frequently about potty training is "Should boys stand or sit?" (I am also asked if the special child-size urinals are worth the investment. They're not!)

To start, sitting is always the best option. It is far less messy, and it is simpler. When sitting, your child has only one thing to focus on, whereas when standing they have to think about urinating as well as aiming. It is also cheaper initially, as you only require one potty. Interestingly, science also tells us that sitting is the best option. Research has found that sitting down allows for improved contraction of the detrusor muscle.[1]

Once boys are potty trained reliably, one of the best ways to practice standing to pee is when you're outside without a quick inside alternative. In a private spot in your backyard, for example. This provides a natural progression to standing when they needed to pee at home, without the need for any specific training. Aim is an issue with young boys, but, once again, this is something that should improve naturally with age (although some men still apparently struggle!). A good way to improve aim when little boys stand is to encourage them to pee onto a Ping-Pong ball floating in the toilet. But if your child's aim does not improve with time, it is worth visiting your doctor to check for a condition known as hypospadias, in which the hole through which urine passes is not at the tip of the penis. This naturally causes problems with aim.

Rewarding success on the potty

One of the keys to gentle potty training is working with your child at a time that is developmentally appropriate. Fundamental to this is understanding that if your child is ready, there is no need for a reward, ever. For this reason, rewards play no role in gentle potty training.

This concept—the absence of rewards—is so alien to mainstream

> If your child is ready, there is no need for a reward, ever.

potty training that I feel it is important to delve a little deeper into the reasons behind it. Whenever we do anything in life, no matter how old we are, we do it for one of two reasons: either because we genuinely want to do it—because it makes us or others feel good (which, in turn, makes us feel good again), or because we are rewarded or punished for doing/ not doing it. You will notice that I've put reward and punishment under the same point and not separated them. This is because they are one and the same. The absence of a reward can be deemed punishment, and vice versa.

When it comes to mainstream potty training, rewards are the mainstay, be it a chocolate candy every time the child has "produced" or a bigger present when they are reliably dry and the diapers have totally disappeared. Often, parents also punish children for accidents when potty training— sometimes without even realizing that they are doing so. Shouting and reprimanding are common when a child wets or soils themselves, the parents' belief being that the child has the ability to be continent but for some reason has de- cided not to be—maybe because they are being naughty or manipulative.

When parents reward or punish potty-training behavior there is a presupposition that their child has full ability, both physiologically and psychologically. This is grossly incorrect. If you need to bribe a child to use the potty with rewards, they are not fully ready, either in mind or in body. And if the child has an accident, punishing them suggests that it was consciously controlled by them, when, in fact, it is an indication that they are not totally ready, whether physiologically or psychologically.

I think most parents understand that punishment is an ineffective potty-training strategy, but rewarding is commonly seen as the way to go. While you may be able to bribe a child into producing a pee or a poo on the potty if you dangle a carrot (or, in this case, a chocolate candy) over their head, the process is a shallow one. You have not truly taught continence. The child is producing while the reward is being offered. They are not learning to listen to their body. Rewards in such circumstances pose two risks: First, children may learn to override their bodily sensations to receive a treat (which is totally counterproductive to the process of potty training); second, as is well-known in psychology, rewards undermine intrinsic, or internal, motivation in children.[2] This means that when the reward is removed, the child is less likely to repeat the behavior—in this case using the potty or the toilet—because they never made the choice to do it in the first place.

Rewards and especially punishment have no place in a mindful, informed, and gentle approach to potty training. If rewards or punishments need to be used, it means that the time is not right. Once the child is ready—in body and in mind—no incentives, or, indeed, disincentives, are needed.

Praising success on the potty

If rewards are counterproductive in gentle potty training, does the same go for praise?

Too much praise and praise that is superficial and shallow are known to lessen intrinsic motivation.[3] Unfortunately the mainstream approach to potty training heaps on the superficial praise. Shouts of "Good boy!," "Well done!," and "Clever girl!" abound, with parents not understanding that this can affect how their child learns to listen to their body's cues. For example, they might sit on the potty and then decide, having paid attention to the sensations in their body, that they don't need to go after all. They will receive no praise in this case, yet this attention to their own bodily needs is an important achievement too, and a necessary part of the process.

So is all potty-training praise misguided? No, there is a kind that can be very helpful: that which is *effort-based* and *specific*—that is, praise that focuses on the child's attempts, no matter the outcome, and tells them specifically what they did that is good. Praise that is descriptive is also very effective. Here are some examples of each:

- **Effort-based praise:** "I guess you didn't need to poo after all, but sitting there waiting for a poo to come was a great idea."
- **Specific praise:** "I saw that you took yourself to the potty when you needed to pee; that

made me really proud that you listened to
your body."

- **Descriptive praise:** "Wow, that's a big poo. I can
see some of the corn you had for dinner
yesterday in it; can you?"

I hope that you can spot the differences between these
and the choruses of "Well done" that most often accompany
potty training. These more focused types of praise can be a
very helpful potty-training tool, as they help the child to
recognize and understand the effects of their actions.

To prompt or not to prompt?

Imagine the following scenario: You have just learned a specific
breathing technique in a yoga class—one that helps you to
calm down when you are feeling tense—but your teacher
phones you every twenty minutes or so to check if you are
feeling tense and to remind you to use the breathing technique
if you are. You would soon get pretty annoyed, wouldn't you?
I would most likely hang up the phone after the second or third
call, having perhaps shouted, "Okay, okay! I get it. When I'm
feeling tense I'll try it—you don't need to keep reminding me."

Now imagine how it feels for a child who has just begun
potty training to hear you asking, "Do you need the toilet?
Are you sure? Do you want to try to squeeze a little one
out?" Constantly prompting is not a great idea.

In chapter 1 we looked at bladder capacity. For most children of potty-training age this is around 200 to 227 ml (or one third of a pint). That's quite a lot of liquid! Interestingly, most toddler cups hold around 230 ml, so in terms of bladder capacity, your child will need a pee for every cup or two of fluid that they drink. (Remember, some of the water is absorbed by the body—not all will be excreted.) It is therefore very important to be realistic when it comes to your expectations of when your child might actually need a pee; otherwise you will be like that annoying yoga teacher. Asking your child if they need a pee no more than once an hour is appropriate— and asking them when you need one yourself, taking their potty into the toilet with you if there is space, is a great idea.

Most children of potty-training age poo once or twice a day. You are at an advantage here, as you are most likely familiar with your own child's bowel habits. If you're lucky, they will poo at a similar time each day, giving you a rough idea of when to expect it to happen sans diapers.

Ultimately, though, unless your child indicates to you verbally that they need a pee or a poo, your best bet is to watch for signs. These are different for every child, but there are some that are quite universal.

Signs of needing a pee:

- Holding the genitals
- Squeezing the legs together tightly

- Crossing the legs
- Fidgeting and squirming
- Hopping from foot to foot

Signs of needing a poo:

- Passing lots of wind
- Holding the tummy
- Hiding behind the sofa (or a similar concealed area)
- Straining and grunting (late stage)

If you notice any of these signs, say to your child, "It looks like you might need to go to the toilet. Let's go and sit on the potty." In the case of grunting and straining, it is sometimes better to quickly put the potty underneath them, as this is a late-stage sign and they may not make it there themselves. Bringing it to them is usually much more successful in this case.

If you don't notice signs of needing a pee, your child has not had one for more than an hour, *and* a sippy cup full of water or milk has been consumed since their last pee, then it would be sensible to prompt them. If, on the other hand, it has been less than an hour (or longer, but they have drunk very little since their last pee), then wait until you spot any cues, you go to the toilet yourself and invite them to join you, or they take themselves to the potty independently.

THE FIRST DAY

Here's a quick recap of what your first day of potty training will look like, step by step:

1. At the start of the day tell your child that you are so excited to begin, that you really trust them to use the potty and can't wait to see how proud they will be of themselves when they do a pee or a poo in it. Explain to them what will happen and ask if they have any questions.

2. Prepare your living area, put down a waterproof sheet to protect the floor, lift up any precious rugs, and consider covering the sofa or chair that your child usually sits on. Put the potty out ready for use, asking them where they would prefer it to be (better still if they put the potty in place themselves).

3. Make sure you have toilet paper and wipes to hand, as well as whatever you need to clean up any spills. Prepare your hand-washing area, and make sure your child understands how to wash their hands and the importance of hygiene.

4. Dress your child from the waist up only, so that they are totally bare-bottomed until bedtime (when you can put a diaper back on). If it is cold, consider using leg warmers.

5. Keep an eye out for early pee and poo cues, prompting them if you see any of these and they don't seem to be taking themselves off to the potty or telling you that they need to go. Be ready to run and put the potty underneath them if you see any straining or hear grunting.

6. When you go to the toilet yourself, invite your child along and bring their potty. If there is not enough space in the bathroom itself, leave the door open and pop the potty at the entrance in a position where you and your child can see each other clearly. Encourage them to sit on the potty while you sit on the toilet—"just like Mommy" or "just like Daddy" (at this stage dads really need to sit down to wee too)—and ask them, "Do you need to do anything in your potty now?" Make sure you describe to them what you are doing while you go (no matter how silly you feel).

7. If they haven't shown any cues and you haven't visited the toilet yourself for an hour, then it is time to prompt them if they have had at least a drinking cup of water or milk. Ask them, "Do you need to have a pee? You haven't been for a while."

8. When they do have a pee or a poo, don't forget your specific and descriptive praise: "Wow, that was a big pee—look how much is in the potty!" or "You did a poo in the potty! Are you proud of yourself?" If they sit on the potty of their own accord but don't do anything, say to them, "I saw you sat on the potty and tried really hard to do a [pee/poo]. I'm so proud of you for really trying hard." Remember—effort-based praise is key.

9. After a pee or a poo, take them to the hand-washing station and encourage them to wash their hands as independently as possible.

Wiping and emptying the potty

In chapter 3 we discussed wipes versus toilet paper. Other than when your child has had a poo that requires extra cleaning or has had an accident, now is the time to switch to toilet paper. Make sure that you keep a roll next to the potty. If your child has had a pee, encourage them to wipe them- selves using the toilet paper and resist the urge to step in and help too soon—the more they do independently, the better. Boys can have a little shake instead of wiping if they prefer.

If they have had a poo, then you are probably going to want to get involved, unless you can cope with a lot of mess. One way to compromise here is to let them take over when you have pretty much finished wiping, which gives them some important autonomy without poo being smeared everywhere. It is quite common for parents to have to take over wiping poos for several months down the line. In fact, it is unusual for children to wipe adequately alone (to the level where underwear isn't covered in poo) before they are around four or five.

Emptying the potty should also be a joint task as much as possible. At the very least, your child should accompany you to the toilet if you aren't brave enough to let them carry the potty. Talk to them about where the pee or poo and toilet paper are going—children are often scared of the toilet flush, and helping them to understand what happens when you flush is an important step toward them sitting on the big toilet in the future. You should also encourage your child to say "bye-bye" to their pee or poo, as this helps them to have positive feelings about their body waste, which may reduce the likelihood of problems such as withholding, wetting, and soiling further down the line. Last, and most important, make sure that you never say things like "yuck," "pooey," "smelly," or "dirty" when they are on their potty, wiping, or emptying the potty. The whole process should be positive; they must never view themselves and their pee or poo as dirty or disgusting. Once again, this can help to reduce the chances of toileting problems in the future.

When accidents happen

Potty training is a learning process, just like any other, and whenever we learn we make mistakes. In fact, potty training and accidents go hand in hand, teaching children about when to hold on and wait and when to go to the toilet as quickly as possible. Accidents teach them to recognize the different sensations within their body and what happens when they respond to or ignore them. These episodes can feel stressful and demoralizing, but only if you let them. Potty accidents are important, not a setback, so try embracing them. Changing your mind-set and your expectations can remove a lot of the stress.

> Potty accidents are important, not a setback.

What to expect

For the first couple of days you can expect more on the floor than in the potty (which is why I stress the importance of protecting your floors and arming yourself with cleaning materials). This is unlikely to change until day three of training, and there will still probably be a few accidents a day for a good few weeks to come.

How should you react to accidents?

First, stay calm. Remember that your child is learning and mistakes are inevitable. Your friend's child may have potty trained in three days with no accidents, but they are the exception to the rule. Don't judge your child's experience against others', especially those that are not realistic or the norm.

Empathize with your child and reassure them that it's okay, that you are not angry, and that everybody makes mistakes. Effort-based praise is important here too: "Oops, you didn't make it to the potty on time. That's okay, you're still learning. I saw that you tried to make it; that was a great thing to do. Next time you'll know to go a bit earlier."

Never, ever shout at or chastise your child for an accident— you could unwittingly cause problems for the future if they link potty training with fear or anxiety. If you're feeling particularly short-tempered and at the end of your tether, leave the room. Take a few deep breaths and tell yourself, "They are learning, this is normal, it's okay," before responding to your child.

As far as possible—or rather, as much as you can cope with—invite your child to help you to clean up the accident. Once again, try as hard as you can to not refer to it as "messy," "smelly," or "dirty," as this sort of talk can make accidents worse by instilling a sense of shame in your child. Allowing them to help you to clean up any accidents can encourage them to develop a sense of ownership, which can aid their learning process. Perhaps they can have a special job of squirting some floor cleaner whenever they have an accident, although this should never be seen as a form of punishment— it's simply helping to tidy up after themselves, just as they would if they spilled a drink or left their toys out.

How long will potty training take?

You may have noticed that I suggested a rough timeline for accidents in the previous section. However, it is impossible to provide an exact one for the process as a whole. Although many experts promise potty training in a week, or even in three days, all children are individuals and will achieve continence in their own time. While some may genuinely be totally dry within three days, they are a tiny minority, and most will continue to have accidents for several weeks, months, and even years down the line.

Having said that, a very rough guide in terms of daytime continence could look something like this:

Day 1: Most on the floor, not in the potty
(bare-bottomed)

Day 2: A 60/40 floor/potty ratio (bare-bottomed)

Day 3: A 50/50 floor/potty ratio (underwear and possibly clothing introduced here)

Day 4: Floor/potty ratio moving toward 40/60

Day 5: Floor/potty ratio moving toward 30/70

Day 6: Floor/potty ratio moving toward 20/80

Days 7–14: Floor/potty ratio moving toward 10/90

The 10/90 ratio (10 percent on the floor or in underwear and 90 percent in the potty) is likely to continue for at least a month or two. After this, the odd accident remains common in the first year after potty training. This is normal, as are regressions (chapter 6 looks at these common problems in detail), and will be outgrown as your child approaches school age. Consistent night continence, however, will take much longer to achieve (see chapter 5).

Leaving the house

You may have looked at this rough timeline with horror. When are you ever going to be able to leave the house? Are you going to be a prisoner in your own home for two weeks? In short, the answer is no. But I would recommend that you try to stay home, if at all possible, until day three at least, and ideally, day four or five. I suggest aiming for more than 50 percent in the potty before venturing out; otherwise your outing is going to be incredibly stressful. Obviously you'll also need to have progressed to a point where your child is wearing underwear and clothing. If they have only previously been bare-bottomed, it is understandable that not only going out of the house but wearing clothes for the first time when training may well lead to disaster.

When you do leave the house, make sure that you take enough changes of clothing with you (this will depend on how long you will be away from home). Initially, I would also recommend that you take your regular potty with you, unless your child has already become familiar with a travel potty. Using a travel potty for the very first time when away from home can exacerbate what is already a potentially traumatic experience for your child. Getting them used to the travel potty at home first is usually much more successful.

Your approach when out of the house remains much the same: Encourage your child to join you whenever you go to the toilet yourself, which you may want to do more regularly when away from home, as it gives you both privacy. Aim to visit the toilet around once an hour, which means that there is no need to prompt as you did at home. Also, watch for cues, although these may be harder to spot when you are out of the house, particularly if you are at a playgroup and your child is engrossed in what they are doing. Last, once again, keep an eye on how much your child is drinking and whether they may be due to have a poo soon. If they need to go and it is not possible to get to a public toilet in time, try to choose a spot that is as secluded as possible, not only for the benefit of others but for your child and yourself too. Using the potty in a place that is fairly hidden from view will give your child the privacy that they may need, particularly if they need a poo. And you will feel less pressure if others cannot see you.

If accidents occur, try to stay calm. It can feel very stressful if they happen with other people watching—which they invariably do. But nobody is judging you, no matter how you may feel. Remember, all parents have been through this, and the chances are that anybody staring at you is thinking back to when the same thing happened to them. Try to ignore bystanders and calmly empathize with your child, getting them cleaned up as quickly and calmly as possible. Keep reminding yourself that accidents are common and normal.

Finally, make sure you take plenty of wipes and a toilet paper roll with you (don't rely on toilet paper stock in public toilets; there will never be any when you need some) and a waterproof bag to put wet and dirty clothes in.

Traveling in the car

Until your child is reliably dry in the daytime, I recommend that you purchase a piddle pad to protect your child's seat when traveling in the car. This is simply a pad that soaks up wee—much like a mattress protector, but car-seat-size. It can also be used in strollers.

Once again, taking your child's potty with you is

generally most successful, allowing you to simply pull over at the side of the road if your child needs to go to the toilet. As they get a little older and more competent at potty training you may want to consider alfresco pees at the side of the road, standing or squatting. For slightly older children, usually aged three or four onward, there are several devices on the market that are specifically made for car toileting. These are gender-specific, as they are shaped specifically for boys' and girls' anatomy (see page 179 for examples).

Day care and different parental homes

I am frequently asked by parents about how to cope with potty training when the child is in day care during the week. As discussed on page 45, you will ideally have allocated a block of between three and seven days at home with your child. Seven days is great, as that means the bulk of the potty training (and also accidents) will happen at home with you. Three days should, however, get you to a point where your child is using the potty at least as often as they are having accidents.

The most important thing to consider when your child returns to day care is that the staff adopt exactly the same approach as the one you have been using at home. It is absolutely key that they do not put your child in diapers again to prevent accidents—this would be a huge step back for the child, not to mention incredibly confusing.

Of course, the best way to avoid potential issues is preparation. Request a meeting with your child's caretaker before you start potty training and fill them in on the method you will be using, making sure to tell them that you do not want them to put your child in diapers when they return. On the first day back after starting potty training fill in the staff on your progress, note any cues you have observed, and give them an idea of how frequently your child needs to use the potty, as well as any triggers for accidents. Also, pack several pairs of clean trousers and underwear (I would suggest four of each for a full day, and at least one change of top) to leave with your day-care provider; it is quite common for more accidents to occur at day care than at home, due to the extra stimulation and their attention shifting away from potty training a little. The extra accidents at day care aren't usually indicative of a problem. They are almost all normal and will reduce in time.

This same approach also applies to parents who are not living together, meaning the child is potty trained in two different homes. Ideally, one parent will focus on the training for a week. However, if a child is with one parent for weekdays and the other for weekends, the parent *who is at home the most* will start, if possible. (It is better for the child to spend a full weekend with a parent at home to begin potty training than Monday to Friday if the parent is working.)

Once again, continuity is vital. Both parents need to understand and use the same approach (ideally by sharing this book) to prompting, clothing, accidents, and, most important, not putting the child back into diapers during the daytime.

. . .

As you may have noticed, continuity and calmness are big themes when it comes to gentle potty training, particularly in the early days. Your actions as a parent will have the biggest impact. Far too many parents go into potty training with unrealistic expectations and think that accidents mean that they are doing things wrong or that their child isn't ready. They then switch between different methods of training or perhaps stop altogether for a while.

Similarly, parents often underestimate the impact of their own emotions on the success of potty training. If you feel exhausted, wrung out, angry, and frustrated, your child is likely to pick up on your emotions. Accidents and resistance are then more likely to occur. Taking some time to care for your own needs, both physical and emotional, can make potty training easier for your whole family.

Understanding the normal course of potty training and being aware that this is a learning process in which mistakes are natural will help you to stay consistent. This consistency will allow you to confidently guide your child through their journey to full bowel and bladder control, both in the daytime and, as we will see next, at night.

CHAPTER 5

Nighttime Potty Training

For most children, nighttime training usually follows daytime training. There are always exceptions, though, and chances are you will meet another parent who tells you, "We ditched diapers totally all at once. She was dry in the day and at night within a week of starting." This can make you doubt your approach and your child's abilities, but you must remind yourself that it is not what happens in 99 percent of cases. The vast majority of children will still need diapers at night for several months, often for years, after they stop needing them in the day. This chapter will help you to understand what sort of a timeline to expect and how to approach nighttime training when your child is ready.

When should you toilet train at night?

As you might expect, given the information covered in chapter 2, there is no "right time." It is much better to think of readiness as a range. Some children will train at the lower end of this range, some at the upper end, and either is perfectly fine. It is also important to understand that the age of starting to toilet train at night is not necessarily the age at which you would expect consistent dryness. Bed-wetting remains common and normal for several years after a child is out of diapers at night.

For most children, nighttime training will begin at some point between three and four years of age, usually around six months to a year after daytime continence is achieved, with research showing that the average gap between attaining day and night dryness is ten months.[1]

Scientists from Switzerland found that no children in their study had bladder control at night at one year of age.[2] Between the ages of two and three years, only 20 percent of the children were reliably dry at night, and by the age of five, 90 percent of them were dry at night, indicating a big shift at three and four years of age. These findings are echoed by Brazilian research showing that 83 percent of children were dry at night by age four.[3]

When it comes to nighttime accidents, the same Swiss study also found that around a quarter of boys and a tenth of girls between six and eighteen years of age still had occasional periods of bed-wetting. Further research, which investigated this in more depth, showed nocturnal enuresis occurred less than twice per week and happened in 21 percent of four-year-olds and 8 percent of nine-year-olds.[4] Bed-wetting more than twice per week affected 8 percent of four-year-olds and 1 percent of nine-year-olds. It is estimated that this rate remains throughout adulthood, with between 1 and 2 percent of adults wetting the bed occasionally.

Do these figures surprise you? I remember being quite surprised when I saw them for the first time. I had no idea that bed-wetting was relatively common in adults or that it still happens with some regularity once children have been out of diapers completely for a couple of years. Accidents happen.

Why does nighttime training happen later?

Night continence requires slightly more sophisticated physiological development than daytime training for three main reasons.

1. **Bladder capacity**: As we learned in chapter 2, bladder capacity increases to 227 ml—around half that of an adult—between the ages of three and four, then to 242 ml by the age of five and 256 ml by the age of six. This enlarged bladder capacity aids continence at night. Some children, however, have a smaller functional bladder capacity, meaning that while the bladder may be able to contain 242 to 256 ml, it sends signals to the brain that it is full earlier, when it is not truly full or needing to be emptied.[5] This bladder overactivity may be evident during the night, but not during the day.

2. **Vasopressin secretion:** The secretion of the antidiuretic hormone vasopressin causes the body to reabsorb more water and reduce the production of urine at night. But because this is dependent on a well-established circadian rhythm, which children do not yet have, it may not be as reliable in them as it is in the adult body. As mentioned earlier (see page 5), children who suffer from persistent bed-wetting can have lower-than-average levels of vasopressin in their bodies at night. This is not the only cause of bed-wetting, but it can be a contributory factor.

3. **Sleep arousability:** Ironically, given their frequent night waking, young children may not wake as easily as adults when it comes to sensing the need to go to the toilet. This lowered arousability in response to bodily sensations means that children urinate more in their sleep than adults.

As you can see, all three of these factors once again rely on physiological development. Night continence can therefore be seen as a developmental milestone and one that cannot be rushed. This doesn't mean that there are no psychological influences on potty training at night—there are several, which we will discuss in the next chapter. However, the underlying requirements for night continence are purely physical and will be attained as the child grows older.

What about naps?

If sleep is an issue in achieving night continence, does this mean a child who sleeps in the day will need to be put back into a diaper for nap time? Not necessarily. In fact, it is not something that I would recommend. There are many differences between nighttime and daytime sleep, the most obvious being the sheer length of time spent asleep. If a child naps for an hour or two, it is perfectly possible that their bladder capacity is large enough to contain the urine produced within this time frame. Arousability levels are also likely to be higher during a nap, as the sleep is not usually as deep as it is at night.

While it is probable that your child will have some accidents when they nap, staying diaper-free is important. It sends a very clear message to them that in the daytime they use the potty. At night, when they are in their pajamas, in their bed and it is dark outside, they use diapers. The distinction between day and night is huge. Using a diaper for naps can set back daytime potty training by not providing that same clear distinction.

Signs of night-training readiness

These are the five main indicators that a child is ready for nighttime training:

- They are three or four years of age.
- They are reliably dry in the daytime, with minimal accidents.
- They have been out of diapers in the daytime for six to twelve months.
- They regularly wake with a dry diaper.
- They are strongly resisting their bedtime diaper or requesting to be diaper-free.

The first two points are important if you are going to attempt nighttime training, while the rest are less so. A child may show no particular signs of wanting to lose their bedtime diaper and/or you may still wake to a wet or soiled diaper every morning. In the case of the latter, you should try to ascertain when the pee or the poo took place. Sometimes children go through the night without using their diaper and only fill it in the morning. This is not the same as using it during the night, which would be a clear sign that they are not ready to lose it.

Once you believe that your child is ready to be diaper-free at night, the next step is some simple preparation. This, yet again, is key to the success of nighttime potty training.

Preparation

These simple preparations can greatly reduce potential stress and anxiety for you and your child. You should start making them at least a week (ideally, two weeks) before the first diaper-free night. Some, however, can be made much further in advance.

1. **Change to cloth diapers at night.** Investing in some reusable cloth diapers can really help to prepare your child for nighttime potty training. Disposables are so effective that children do not always realize that they have done something in their diaper. Cloth diapers, on the other hand, prevent clothing and bedding from becoming wet or soiled but retain a small sensation of dampness, which can make a child more aware of when they are using their diaper. The other advantage of switching to cloth diapers at night is that if you select ones that look a little more like underwear, this can help the child feel more grown up and excited about losing the diaper completely at night in the future.

2. **Buy a good mattress protector.** Realistically, nighttime potty training means accidents are going to happen. Protecting your child's mattress (or your own if you are bedsharing) is vital. Look for a fitted-sheet-type mattress protector. The more waterproof the better, but avoid ones that feel too rubbery or plasticky as these can make your child really sweaty and uncomfortable, which can affect their sleep—not a positive start to nighttime training. You may also want to buy some disposable bed mats for extra protection.

3. **Buy a second potty for the bedroom.** If you live in a two- (or more) story house, the ideal would be to have two potties—one for upstairs and one for downstairs. There is nothing worse than your child needing the toilet in the night, only for you to re-member that you have left the potty downstairs. But while the nightly sprint up and down the stairs may be annoying, the real problem is that your child is unlikely to be able to hold on until you return with their potty, meaning accidents are more likely. Even if your home is on one level, it is still worth consid-ering keeping a second potty in your child's bedroom permanently; although you may not have stairs to contend with, the time spent retrieving the potty from another room could be too long for your child to wait. Using a potty in the bedroom is often more successful than taking your child to the toilet, at least temporarily.

4. **Get a good night-light.** Unfortunately, nighttime potty training often coincides with the stage when fear of the dark most commonly sets in with a vengeance. Of course, this doesn't mean all children will be scared, but for those who are, having to get up in the dark can be enough to prevent them from using the potty at night. But even if children aren't scared of the dark, they will need some light to be able to see where the potty is. A good night-light should be bright enough to allow you to clearly see the potty and should be of the wall-plug variety. Although battery-operated portable lights may seem appealing because they can be moved to wherever the potty is, there is also the chance that the batteries might run out at a vital time.

Most important, you should only use a night-light that emits red light. This is the only color wavelength that does not inhibit the body's secretion of melatonin, the sleep hormone. Regular white lights (which actually have a very blue wavelength) cause a huge amount of melatonin inhibition and so can create problems with sleep.

5. **Discuss what will happen.** One advantage of nighttime training taking place with a slightly older child is that their cognitive understanding and language ability are usually significantly greater. This means that you can have a good discussion with them about what is going to happen, how you believe that they are mature enough to sleep without a diaper at night, and how they can achieve that. Starting this talk a week or so before the first diaper-free night can really help to get you off to a good start.

The lifting debate

Many parents approach potty training at night by "lifting" their child before or when they go to bed themselves. This simply means that the child is woken by the parent, taken to the toilet, and encouraged to pee. Often the children are really drowsy, but most will still urinate when prompted. They are then returned to bed.

While lifting can certainly reduce the number of accidents, it is not something that I support. Leaving your child out of diapers at night should be an indication that they are ready to control their bladder at nighttime and take cues from their body if they need to go to the toilet. If both of these happen, there is no need for lifting. It can also be argued that a child who does need it is not one who is ready to be out of diapers at night.

There are also potential pitfalls with lifting. First, you are depriving the child of the chance to notice their own cues, so night continence becomes reliant on lifting and true continence can be delayed. Second, lifting runs the risk of affecting sleep. Most parents have no idea where in a sleep cycle their child is when they wake them to be lifted. Disturbing sleep cycles can cause the circadian rhythm to reset slightly, and this can cause habitual waking, which, in itself, can become problematic.

Rewarding and praising

Just as they have no place in daytime training (see page 59), these have no place at night. If your child needs to be rewarded or showered with praise to no longer use a diaper at night, then the chances are that they are not truly ready to do so. No child has the intention of staying in nighttime diapers forever—the motivation is already there to be diaper-free, both from a comfort perspective and an emotional desire to grow and mature.

Research has shown that there is no significant effect from rewarding a child for night dryness compared to not giving any rewards at all.[6] Rewards do not speed up the process or reduce accidents.

The same is true for outcome-based praise or that which is nonspecific in nature. Remember, any praise should be *specific, descriptive,* and as *effort-based* as possible (see page 62)—something that is particularly hard when your child wakes you at three o'clock in the morning telling you that they need to use the potty!

Should you restrict bedtime fluids?

Many people believe that night dryness will be attained quicker if the child's fluids are restricted in the evening and especially at bedtime. This is a bit of an old wives' tale. There is simply no need to cut back on fluid in the evening, although you should restrict drinks that have a diuretic effect (that is, make the body produce more urine than usual). The major culprits here are carbonated drinks and those containing caffeine—for instance, tea (however weak and milky) and hot chocolate. Some fruits can also have a diuretic effect, due to their levels of potassium, which helps the body to excrete sodium in urine. The most common culprits are melon, bananas, kiwi, apricots, peaches, and avocados. Pineapple is also a natural diuretic, so it should ideally be avoided in both solid and juice form immediately before bedtime.

Getting started on the first night

Once your preparations are well under way and you're sure that this is the right time for your child, you need to pick a night to begin. This first night and the few thereafter are likely to be punctuated with accidents and thus some upheaval. For this reason, I always recommend starting on a Friday night, especially if you work during the week, so that you can recover and catch up on any lost sleep over the weekend.

If you plan to start on a Friday night as I've suggested, a good time to talk about it would be from the Monday before. Explain that once the weekend comes (and they have finished at their school/babysitter/nursery/playgroup for the week), they will be sleeping without their diaper. It is really important that you make this sound as appealing as possible. You could say, for example, "I'm so excited for you to sleep without a diaper at night like I do!" This is also the time to check if your child has any questions or any anxieties. Reassure them that you will help if they wake up in the night and need you and that it's okay for them to come into your room and to tell you, or call out for you (whatever you and they prefer). Also, tell them that it's okay if they have an accident. Explain that it is quite common and nothing to be worried about or ashamed of. If you remember wetting the bed as a child, talk to them about your experience then and how you have learned since. Remind them that it's okay to be a beginner, that you understand that they are learning, and that you absolutely won't get angry if they have an accident.

Getting the bedroom ready on the first night

On Friday, make sure that your child's bedroom is prepared. You could involve them in this if you have time, and talk to them about how exciting it is to be getting everything ready. There are a number of things to remember, some of which you may have done in advance.

- Put the bedroom potty out; choose a place where it is easily found and accessible from your child's bed but not where you'll kick it over in the night.

- Put some toilet paper and wipes out next to the potty (the latter is for you to use should they have an accident).

- Have your chosen cleaning products ready and close at hand.

- Make sure the mattress protector is on the bed and, if you are using disposable bed mats, put these on the bed too.

- Make sure the night-light is plugged in before bedtime and that the potty is visible.

- Make up the bed with several sheets. If (or, more accurately, when) your child has an accident, the last thing you want is to be searching for clean bedding and changing the bed in the middle of the night. Using at least two or three bottom sheets, one fitted over the other with a disposable bed mat in between, means that you can just whip off the wet layer quickly in the night, leaving the bed dry and the new sheet ready to go. This may seem like a lot of work, but it is work you will thank yourself for at three in the morning.

Bedtime

When bedtime comes around, check one last time if your child has any questions and run through what they should do if they need to go to the toilet or if they have an accident. Going to the toilet should be the last thing they do before bedtime, after bathing, teeth brushing, and putting on pajamas, and you should get into the habit of taking them each night. Initially, you may have to prompt, but hopefully, after a few weeks, it will become habitual. The same is true of mornings—encourage your child to go to the toilet as soon as they wake up every day. It should always be the last thing they do before and the first thing they do after sleep.

When accidents happen

As we've established, potty training and accidents go hand in hand. You simply don't get one without the other. And accidents at night, especially in the early days, are inevitable too, going on for months or even years after nighttime potty training in some cases. The key to coping with this is acceptance, along with a good dose of preparation, as we have already covered.

When it comes to bed-wetting, research has shown that boys are twice as likely as girls to be affected.[7] There is no one specific reason for this, although undoubtedly expectations and stereotyping play a role, as mentioned earlier (see page 23). Boys do tend to be night-trained later than girls, so perhaps this delay gives girls a head start.

One thing that certainly does have a biological impact on bed-wetting is genetics, so if you or your partner had frequent accidents as a child, there is a very good chance that your child may do so too. Research has shown that if a child has one parent who was prone to bed-wetting in childhood themselves, then there is a 40 percent chance that they will wet the bed.[8] If both parents used to wet the bed as children, the risk rises to 75 percent. The next chapter will cover common causes of bed-wetting in more detail; the remainder of this chapter will look at the practicalities as well as the emotions surrounding it and what to do when you feel that the problem is too large for you to manage alone.

Reassuring your child when bed-wetting happens

Bed-wetting can be extremely distressing for children, often far more so than wetting during the day. When accidents happen, your goal should be to reassure, normalize, and support. Reassure your child that it's okay to have accidents, explaining that every child does at some point. This is where you might tell your own story of the time (or times) when you wet your bed. Try to recall how you felt when you woke up lying on a wet sheet: "I remember feeling really sad and embarrassed when it happened to me." Then ask how they feel: "Do you feel like that now? Or are you feeling different?" Be sure to tell your child that you're not angry, that it's okay that they had an accident. And reassure them that you still have faith that they are ready and can get through the night. Remind them that they are still learning and that everybody makes mistakes when they learn, but that soon they will get really good at it and the mistakes will stop. You could ask your child if they would like to help you to change their bedding (which should be quite minimal work if you have prepared and made up a few bottom layers—see "Getting the Bedroom Ready on the First Night" on page 92) or to put the wet sheets in the washing machine. It's okay if they choose not to help you, though. Finally, encourage your child to go to the toilet or potty with you, before they get back into bed. Often the bladder is not completely emptied when bed-wetting occurs, so they may still need to go. When you leave their room, remind your child what to do if they wake up and need the toilet and end by telling them that you love them and are proud of them for trying so hard. (Remember that effort-based praise is far more important than outcome-based praise.)

Handling your own emotions when bed-wetting happens

Bed-wetting can be tough to handle as a parent, not least because it happens at night when you are normally asleep yourself. The early days of nighttime toilet training can feel a little like having a newborn baby again, with the interrupted sleep. But just as the night waking in babyhood eventually came to an end, so will the disturbed nights from nighttime potty training. The key to surviving both is in your hands. You cannot make a newborn baby stop waking at night to feed, and you cannot make your child sleep all night without any accidents. You can, however, control how you respond in either situation. Night waking because of accidents or your child needing the toilet can quickly become irritating, and your nerves and temper are likely to be tested to the limit. Undoubtedly, the best way to respond to your child when they need you at night is to stay calm and compassionate, but this will happen only if you work hard on your own emotions and responses.

There is no one right way to stay calm; different things will work for different people. Here are some suggestions that may help if you don't already have a preferred technique:

• Take a deep breath in through your nose to the count of four, then exhale through your nose to a count of eight.

- Close your eyes and imagine a dial in your head that is responsible for your levels of patience. Imagine it turned all the way to the top, in the red warning section, tested to its limits. Now imagine it moving slowly toward the green section, below the 50 percent marker.

- Remind yourself that this is normal and will pass. You could even repeat the following over and over in your mind: "This is normal. It is to be expected, and it will pass."

- Try to put yourself in your child's place. Imagine how they are feeling right now—perhaps scared, anxious, or sad. As soon as you realize that they are probably feeling worse than you, you will find that you naturally become less angry with them.

- If you live with a partner, take turns each night to go to your child and clean up, so that each of you gets a break. Or perhaps one of you can do Monday to Friday and the other take control on weekends.

  If you ever feel yourself losing your temper, it is better

> **Find a way to stay calm, and your child will have an easier time staying calm too.**

for you to delay entering your child's room or to leave it temporarily. Your emotions and subsequent responses really do play a huge role in the success of night training. Find a way to stay calm, and your child will have an easier time staying calm too.

When to seek help

While bed-wetting is normal and common, there does come a point when you may need to seek professional help. Occasional bed-wetting in children under the age of seven is not a cause for concern, especially if it has happened ever since they were potty trained at night (primary nocturnal enuresis). However, if your child is seven or older and the bed-wetting is happening with some frequency (more than once per month), your first port of call should be your family doctor. Similarly, if your child was previously dry at night and the accidents have suddenly started after months or years of dryness (secondary nocturnal enuresis), seeking medical help is advisable.

There are a few underlying medical reasons for persistent bed-wetting, and your doctor will explore these or, most likely, refer you to a specialist. It is important that any underlying reason is treated; that, in turn, should stop the bed-wetting. Sometimes no cause is found, though this doesn't mean nothing can be done. There are several treatment options available, and these, along with the conditions commonly linked to persistent bed-wetting, are discussed in the next chapter.

Nighttime potty training can seem like a daunting prospect—far more so than training in the daytime. Many parents put it off for fear of how and when to begin, but if losing diapers is well planned from a time perspective and you have prepared effectively, then it should not be too arduous. Accidents will happen, but knowing how to respond will empower you and your child so that the road to night continence is stress-free.

CHAPTER 6

Common Problems and How to Solve Them

Whether you have followed this book since the beginning of your child's potty-training journey and have hit a few bumps, or you have already trained your child using other methods and are now struggling with specific issues, this chapter is for you. Here we will look at the most common potty-training problems, their causes, and, most important, what you can do to resolve them. I have subdivided the problems into "Pee" and "Poo" sections, but in fact many problems have similar root causes. For this reason, I would recommend that you read the whole of this chapter, even if you have only one specific concern.

Pee problems

We have already covered how to cope with wetting accidents in the previous two chapters, so in this section I will focus on their most common causes, especially when they are persistent or start after fairly long periods of continence. I will also look at something that hardly any other potty-training book touches on: What happens if your child withholds pees or totally refuses to do them on the potty? Let's start there.

Withholding and potty refusal

There are five main reasons children withhold pees or refuse to use the potty. Some are purely physiological in origin and some psychological; often, they can be a mix of both.

• **Starting training too soon** Beginning potty training too soon can undermine your child's confidence. After some time, the lack of success can become a huge problem. The child will often try to avoid making mistakes or having accidents by refusing to go to the toilet for as long as possible, saving wees for when you put their nappy on at bedtime. As I've said, once you have started potty training, you really should resist putting your child back into diapers. However, if they are withholding and you feel that you may have started potty training too soon, this is one of only a handful of occasions when I would advocate putting them back into diapers temporarily and trying again when the timing is more biologically appropriate.

- **Pain and fear of pain** If your child is experiencing pain while urinating or has done in the past, they may try to withhold their pee for as long as possible in order to postpone the pain. The most common cause of this is a urinary-tract infection (UTI—see page 112), although yeast infections can cause pain too. Sometimes, however, pain can be caused by catching themselves in their fly while unzipping or zipping their trousers up or from pressure in delicate places from the potty. The solution here is to check for any obvious causes of discomfort and eliminate them as much as possible; it may also involve a trip to your family doctor. Sometimes the memory of pain can also cause issues with potty refusal because of the association. In this case, you should reassure your child as much as possible that it shouldn't hurt anymore. You can do this by encouraging them to pee in the bath or shower, as the warm water can help to diminish any pain, or to sit on the potty fully clothed (as a seat, not to pee). Once they realize the pain has gone, the refusal should disappear.

- **Asserting control** There are only three aspects of their lives that a child is able to completely control—sleeping, eating, and going to the toilet: You can put them to bed, but you cannot make them sleep; you can put food in their mouth, but you cannot make them swallow; and you can sit them on the potty or toilet, but you cannot make them do anything. A child who is feeling a lack of autonomy over their own life will commonly try to assert as much control as possible in one or all of these areas. Giving them more control over what they wear, what they eat, how they spend their days, what and who they play with, and so on can have a very positive effect on toilet withholding. If children have adequate control over their own lives on a day-to-day basis, they won't feel the need to assert it when it comes to going to the toilet.

- **Fear and anxiety around repercussions** Children often withhold pee if they are scared of the repercussions of accidents. A child who has been shouted at, punished in some way, or embarrassed in front of siblings or peers for wetting may try to avoid going to the toilet at all, in case they get something else wrong. These repercussions may not have been at home—often they are at day care or school. If your child is withholding and they are not with you during the day, then you should start with a conversation with whoever looks after them during the day. The same is true of children with separated parents. Withholding is quite often a clue that all is not right in one of the places where the child spends their time.

Sometimes children also withhold out of performance anxiety, rather than any fear of repercussions. Self-confidence is a huge issue here—and it may not be solely related to toilet training but a more general issue. Praise plays a huge role here. In chapter 4 we looked at the implications of ineffective praise and how to make it more specific and effective (see page 62). If you believe self-confidence may be playing an issue, rereading that discussion is a good place to start. Also, be careful not to compare your child to other children, your own or others. Remember that your child is unique, and so is their potty-training journey—comparing them to others and, especially, others' achievements and lack of setbacks, will only serve to undermine their self-confidence further.

• **Insufficient hydration** So far we have looked of causes of withholding and refusal where the child actually needs to go to the toilet but avoids it for some reason. What if they don't actually need to go, though? The most common cause for infrequent urination is a lack of or dramatically lowered fluid intake. Sometimes this can also happen if the weather is very hot and the child is dehydrated. Making sure that your child is adequately hydrated is really important. If their body doesn't have enough fluid, then it will desperately try to hold on to what it does have. Contrary to popular belief, there is no specific amount of fluid to consume each day. The ideal amount varies from person to person and situation to situation. The best way to tell if your child is adequately hydrated is to check the color of their pee, although this is obviously difficult if they are not urinating very often. It should be a very pale straw color— any darker than this and they are dehydrated and should be urged to drink more liquids until things return to normal.

Wetting during the day

When talking about wetting during the day, it is important to distinguish between that which started in the early days of potty training and hasn't improved (primary enuresis) and that which began after a stretch of continence (secondary enuresis). These different types of wetting often have very different causes, so it's important to consider whether they are more likely primary or secondary enuresis.

• **Starting training too soon** If training has begun too soon, the child will struggle to read their own body cues and take themselves to the potty, so accidents are likely to happen. Primary enuresis will almost always occur in such cases. While it is possible to start potty training early, if you constantly prompt the child or use a trigger word or noise while moving the child to the potty, this is not true continence. Constant prompting or cueing could result in their struggling to take themselves to the potty of their own accord in the future. The aim of true continence is for the child to be aware of their bodily sensations and have complete control of them—that means going to the toilet when necessary and holding on when this is not possible. The key message here is to not be in a rush to potty train properly. When the child is capable of true continence there will be far fewer mistakes.

- **Training moving too quickly** Another cause of primary enuresis is the parent (or other caregivers) trying to hurry the process. This could mean rushing to move on to underwear or clothing too soon or trying to speed up the move to the big toilet if your child has trained initially on the potty. The answer here is simply to slow things down. When you rush to finish potty training quickly, it can often end up taking longer.

- **Too much or not enough prompting** Under- or overprompting can also contribute to primary enuresis. As we've seen, to potty train successfully, children need to learn to read their body's cues and signals and to act on them in time. Overprompting—constantly asking if they need to go to the toilet—doesn't teach this. In fact, it may have the opposite effect, as they may stop listening to you and, in turn, to their bodies, making accidents more likely. But underprompting can be an issue too. It is quite common for a child to miss their body's cues in the early days, especially if they are engrossed in an activity. Adult prompting can help them to focus more on their body. I suggest prompting hourly (see page 64)—this should reduce accidents by helping children to tune in to their body's cues, while not bombarding or irritating them.

- **Concentration and play** Have you ever been engrossed in a film, a book, or a conversation and put off going to the toilet in order to finish what you were doing? This is a situation young children find themselves in on an almost daily basis. If a child is absorbed by an activity, wetting is quite common. (This applies to both primary and secondary enuresis, although it tends to occur more with primary.) As adults, we recognize our point-of-no-return sensations and know when we absolutely can't hold on anymore, whatever we are doing. But many children lack the experience and/or the physical maturity to do this, and even if they do catch themselves in time, they will often wet themselves en route to the toilet. Holding it is a learned skill—in other words, accidents will stop in time. Until this happens, try to keep an eye on your child for early signs of needing the toilet whenever they become involved in an activity. If you notice a sign that you think they have missed or are ignoring, say, "Do you need to go to the toilet? Don't worry, we can do it quickly and you won't miss out on your play."

- **Location of potty or toilet** In your own home, the location of your child's potty can have a big impact on the success of training in the early days. If your child has too far to travel to reach it, accidents are almost inevitable. The same applies to the toilet when they transition to it. So if your toilet is on a different floor than your main living area, consider using a potty for a little while longer. The trip upstairs can cause accidents if your child waits too long; they also tend to be less likely to take themselves off to the toilet if it is on a different level in the house, if you have other children, or are occupied, and it is inevitable that your child will need to go to the toilet alone at some point.

Location of the potty or toilet can also play a big role in secondary enuresis. A child who is reliably dry at night at home may well have an accident if you are visiting friends or family and don't ensure that they know where the toilet or potty is. If you are busy talking and your child doesn't feel able to interrupt you to ask you to take them to the toilet, the chances are that they will wet themselves rather than try to find where to go independently. If this occurs, it is not their fault—it is your omission and over-sight. I cannot stress enough how important it is if you are visiting friends or family and your child is not very fa-miliar with their home that you find the toilet and show them where to go, ahead of when it's needed. This should be an absolute priority as soon as you arrive.

• **Complicated clothing** Whether your child has been potty trained for six days or six months, the clothing they wear can have a big impact on their ability to go to the toilet quickly and independently. Try to remember the last time you were desperate to go to the toilet but had to fumble with a belt buckle, complicated buttons, or a stuck zipper. If you, as an adult, might struggle to remove your clothing quickly enough to go to the toilet, it is understandable that a child might have an accident in the same circumstances.

Potty-friendly clothing remains important until your child is both a potty-training pro and an undressing and dressing pro. If they find belts, dungarees, stiff zippers, or proper buttons (as opposed to snaps) difficult, try to avoid them for the time being.

- **Anxiety and change** If a child is anxious and coping with big transitions in their life, secondary enuresis may appear. This is particularly true of any situation where they feel a lack of control over what is happening to them; for instance, starting a new nursery, preschool, or school, or even going away on vacation.

  The most common scenario that can leave a child feeling out of control, anxious, and facing a huge, unsettling change is when a new baby arrives. The appearance of a new sibling can be an incredibly difficult transition for young children, whether they are two or five years old (and any age in between). Toileting regressions are not uncommon, therefore, in new big brothers or sisters. Many people will say that the child is wetting themselves "for attention" or because "they are jealous of the new baby." In reality, the child is most likely feeling very anxious about your love for them (after all, if you loved them, why would you want another child? Do you want to replace them? Are they not enough for you?) and their place in your home. As hard as parents try, attention is inevitably diverted away from the older sibling, and many can go from having had 100 percent of their attention to less than 50 percent overnight. Rather than jealousy, I believe the feeling that new big brothers or sisters experience is more akin to grief. Is it any wonder then that these feelings of grief, uncertainty, anxiety, and a lack of control over what is happening in their lives cause toilet accidents? Also, being a "big boy" or a "big girl" might not seem so appealing anymore when the new baby—the one who has all the attention—is wearing diapers; perhaps children in diapers get more attention than those in underwear?

If you find yourself in this situation, the best thing you can do is to stay compassionate and supportive toward your child. Realize what a difficult transition they are going through, reassure them that you love them as much as ever, support them when they cry or get angry, and spend as much one-on-one time with them as possible, away from the baby. Most important, stay calm when they have accidents. Try to remind yourself that they are not doing it deliberately to annoy you; they are doing it because they are emotionally hurting. This phase will pass naturally once emotional equilibrium is restored.

• **Physiological problems** There are two main physiological problems that can cause wetting accidents, both primary and secondary. These are urinary tract infections (UTIs) and constipation. UTIs have an obvious link to problems with pee. Constipation does not, yet it can be a huge and common issue. When a child is severely constipated, the impacted poo in their colon and rectum slowly increases in mass until it becomes too large and too solidified to pass. The pressure from the sheer size of this mass presses on the bladder, causing the child to lose some control of it. This is an important and frequently undiagnosed problem, and we will return to it in more detail on page 119.

UTIs are fairly common in children and, although not usually very serious, they can have quite a dramatic impact on bladder control. UTIs can affect the upper urinary tract, which includes the kidneys and the ureters (the ureters being the tubes that connect the bladder and the kidneys) or the lower urinary tract, which includes the bladder and the urethra. Bladder infections are often known as cystitis. UTIs often present with a fever, irritability, loss of appetite, and lethargy. Children with UTIs tend to experience pain when they pee, which can cause them to withhold it, or they may pee more frequently and often uncontrollably, causing accidents. Their pee might also smell funny or look cloudy, but not necessarily. If you suspect that your child has a UTI, your first port of call should be your family doctor, who will normally ask for a sample in order to confirm a diagnosis and prescribe appropriate antibiotics. If your child has secondary enuresis, then medical issues or specifically UTIs and constipation should always be ruled out first.

Wetting at night

Just as with wetting during the day, night wetting has several causes, many of which are the same. Night wetting is referred to as either primary nocturnal enuresis or secondary nocturnal enuresis and, as with daytime wetting, "primary" means that the issues have existed from the start of nighttime potty training, while "secondary" means that the issues are new, coming after a long period of reliable night dryness.

Let's now look at some of the causes of night wetting. Where these are the same as for daytime wetting, I have cross-referenced to avoid repetition.

- **Genetics** As discussed on page 94, bed-wetting has a strong genetic component. If either parent wet the bed as a child, there is a significantly increased risk that their child may do so too. If both parents were bed-wetters, the risk that their child will do the same is high. Unfortunately, in most cases the only solution is time. But if your child is over seven years of age and still wetting with regularity, a visit to your family doctor to ask for a referral to a pediatric urologist should be your first step.

- **Small functional bladder capacity and overactive bladders** Bed-wetting can also be linked to the capacity and function of the bladder. As mentioned in chapter 5, children who regularly wet the bed may have a reduced functional bladder capacity—that is, their bladder is usually the same size as the norm, but it holds less urine before it sends a message to the brain that the child needs to wee. With an overactive bladder, the detrusor muscle fails to relax completely while the bladder is filling, and this almost constant contraction prevents the bladder from reaching its full capacity. Research has found that between 70 and 80 percent of those affected by nocturnal enuresis have a degree of detrusor muscle instability.[1] This condition necessitates medical advice and most likely a multidisciplinary approach to treatment. Your first contact should once again be your family doctor.

- **Starting night-time potty training too soon** See page 106 in the daytime wetting section.

- **Fear of the dark** Many young children, especially those aged between three and five, struggle with fear of the dark. This is a common age for a fear of monsters, ghosts, and other things that go bump in the night to emerge. If a child is scared of the dark, they are less likely to get up to visit the potty in their own bedroom. But if the potty is not in their bedroom, or they need to wake you for help, the walk from their room to yours can also be fraught with anxiety—if there is insufficient lighting, for example. In the previous chapter we looked at the importance of a good but sleep-friendly light source to stay on all night in your child's bedroom (see page 87), but you should also think about lighting in your hallway. Lighting the space between your child's bedroom and yours, and between your child's room and the bathroom, can help to reduce their fear and may also mean a reduction in night wetting.

- **Anxiety and change** See page 110 in the daytime wetting section.

- **Too much diuretic food and drink before bed** In chapter 5 we looked at various foods and drinks and their potential diuretic effect—that is, their tendency to increase the production of urine. If your child is regularly consuming food or drink with a diuretic effect at bedtime or immediately before, then there is a distinct possibility that it could be impacting nighttime wetting. Here, though, it is important to remember that fluids (without a diuretic effect) should not be withheld before bedtime. Withholding fluids can lead to constipation, which is one of the leading causes of wetting accidents, both in the daytime and at night (see page 119).

- **Not visiting the toilet before bed** If children do not get into the habit of visiting the toilet or using their potty immediately before bedtime, they are far more likely to need the toilet in the night and thus more likely to wet the bed. Visiting the toilet should become as habitual as teeth brushing; it should be the very last thing that your child does before getting into bed, every single night.

- **UTIs and constipation** See page 112 in the daytime wetting section and page 119.

Poo problems

As demoralizing as pee problems may be, there is no doubt that poo problems are often far more stressful, for both parent and child. If any aspect of potty training is going to stretch your patience to the limit, it is most likely to be problems with poo. And if you are not careful, these issues can go on for many months and even years. The quicker you identify the cause of the problems, the quicker you can work on a solution and reduce the risk of their recurring or getting worse at a later date.

The remainder of this section will look at some common poo problems, their causes, and potential solutions.

Withholding

Some children hold their poo for as long as possible, refusing to go when it is obvious to you that they need to. There are four main reasons why this occurs:

- **Pain** Most cases of poo withholding stem from pain, either current or the memory of it. This is particularly true if the child is suffering from chronic constipation. Once a child links the idea of having a poo with pain, a vicious cycle can begin; they withhold for fear of the pain that accompanies having a poo, but withholding makes the constipation worse, ultimately making the pain worse when they do eventually manage to go. This cycle must be broken, both from the perspective of eliminating the constipation (see page 119) and reducing the child's anxiety because of the pain. There are some good books that can help to alleviate the anxiety (see page 178 for recommendations). Some children also need referrals for therapy if the constipation and resulting pain are particularly severe. Your family doctor should be able to help here.

- **Fear and anxiety** While fear of pain is undoubtedly the top cause of children withholding poo from an emotional perspective, other fears can also come into play. Fear of sitting on an adult toilet can often cause issues with poo. To a child, the toilet can seem like a big, scary place, especially when the flush is activated and the poo is sucked away with a big whoosh. Understandably, they can fear being sucked away into the toilet too, and this then leads to toilet avoidance, which can lead to issues with constipation and pain. Fear and anxiety can also come into play if the child has had previous accidents and has been treated in a rather harsh way. This fear of messing up again can cause them to try to withhold poo so they don't find themselves in the position of having another accident. They are not deliberately refusing to poo to irritate you; there is always an underlying fear or anxiety, and it is this that needs to be uncovered and worked with. Once again, starting with books or videos produced specifically with children in mind is a great idea (see page 178 for recommendations). Some children will, however, benefit from some specialized therapy with a mental health professional.

- **Lack of privacy** How would you feel if you had to poo in front of people you didn't know very well? Perhaps your work colleagues? Or the parents waiting at the school gate? I'm guessing you would feel uncomfortable and would do anything possible to hold on, even if you were desperate. Perhaps you would also feel uncomfortable having to poo in front of people you know really well too. Why do we expect things to be different for children? There is a reason why children often disappear off behind a sofa to poo or try to hide in another room. Giving your child as much privacy as they need is really important when it comes to resolving poo refusal or withholding.

• **Constipation** The most important factor at play when it comes to poo refusal or withholding is constipation. In chapter 3 we looked at the importance of preparing your child's diet for potty training. The sad truth is that most children eat too little fiber and drink too little fluid. This is a recipe for constipation. Constipation doesn't just cause withholding and poo refusal; it has a huge impact on every single aspect of potty training and continence and also on behavior. Sadly, it is often mis-diagnosed and poorly treated too, further adding to the problem. Most people believe that the only real signs of constipation are infrequent poos, difficulty or pain when having a poo, and hard poo, often in large forms, when the child finally manages to go. Constipation can, however, masquerade as diarrhea, frequent poos, and often soiling. This is because the hard masses that become impacted cause any further waste to become liquefied or to pass in very small amounts, often like rabbit droppings or ribbons, in order to get past the blockage. This is known as "overflow poo." Diarrhea, therefore, is a common symptom of constipation. Constipation can also affect the bladder, when the mass presses on it, often causing frequent wetting. I cannot stress enough that if you are worried about your child's bowel habits, as well as their bladder, then you must consider constipation as a potential cause.

If you suspect that your child is constipated, your first stop should, once again, be your family doctor, who can refer you to a pediatric gastroenterologist if needed. The specialist may carry out several tests, which may include digital rectal imaging, ultrasounds, and endoscopy. Once the severity of constipation is understood, treatment may include laxatives or enemas in the disimpaction stage (removal of the hard poo blockage), while behavioral interventions and meetings with nutritional therapists usually accompany maintenance treatment. Food intolerances and allergies should also be considered, since they can be a contributing factor. Ongoing maintenance treatment is often necessary, as relapses are fairly common.

Refusal to poo in the toilet or potty

Refusing to poo outside of diapers is slightly different from complete withholding, although fear and anxiety can still play a part if the child associates sitting on the potty or toilet with pain. Anxiety about falling into the toilet and being flushed away can also be at work.

In addition, there are two further factors that can cause refusal to poo out of nappies:

- **A need for more privacy.** The same applies here as to withholding (see page 117), except taking a poo in a diaper allows the child mobility. This means they can hide more easily, especially if they are in their own room at night.

- **A need to have their feet firmly on the floor.** As discussed on page 32, in order to help the anal sphincters to open, the feet need to be on the floor and, ideally, the child should adopt a squatting position. Although many potties facilitate this position to some extent, there are those that don't, and toilets can leave children with their legs dangling (which is why having a step is so important). The child should be able to sit with their feet fully supported and their knees slightly higher than their hips. Wearing a diaper once again gave them mobility and the ability to squat to allow for an easier, more comfortable poo.

How to encourage poos in the potty or toilet

Your main goals when trying to get your child to poo out of diapers is to ensure that there is no physiological discomfort or inhibition, that their emotions are considered, and that any fear and anxiety are allayed. Aside from ensuring that there is no constipation, you can also do the following:

- Help your child to be more accepting of the toilet, with a children's book specifically aimed at using "the big toilet" and/or with books or videos, specifically about using the potty or toilet for poos (see my recommendations on page 178).

- If your child is consistently having a poo in their bedtime diaper, consider night training. Removing all diapers may initially result in some accidents; however, it will reduce reliance on the night diaper and increase the chance of poos on the toilet or potty.

- Give your child a bottle of bubbles to blow while they are sitting on the potty or toilet. Blowing bubbles helps the jaw to relax, which also has an effect on the anal sphincters, enabling them to relax too. It also helps to take their mind off any fear or anxiety surrounding poo time.

- Try putting an open diaper inside your child's potty and encourage them to sit on it (this helps them to get used to pooing in a sitting position, as well as to sitting on the potty); eventually, the diaper can be removed, leaving just the potty.

- If you are using the big toilet, consider using a potty just for poos. Allow them to choose a private place so they can "hide" while having a poo.

- If you see your child beginning to have a poo in their clothing or underwear, encourage them to sit on the potty, even with their underwear on at first if they are less anxious that way. This allows them to get used to the feeling of sitting to poo.

- If your child has a poo accident in their underwear, encourage them to help you to deposit it in the toilet when they are done, making sure you say "bye-bye" to the poo as it is flushed away. A great story to accompany this is *Poo Goes Home to Pooland* (see page 177).

- Consider purchasing a Squatty Potty. This is a specially designed toilet step that allows children to sit in a squatting position that is more physiologically appropriate.

Soiling

What if your problem is not that your child withholds poos or refuses to do them in the potty or on the toilet but that they constantly soil themselves, either during the day in their underwear or at night in their pajamas?

Soiling might initially seem to be unrelated to withholding, but actually there are many similarities. As we look at the main reasons for soiling and how you can help to stop it, we will come across many ideas that have already been covered in this chapter. This is no coincidence. Most toileting accidents stem from only a few small causes; namely, starting training too soon, constipation, or emotional upset. Let's consider these same causes now in relation to soiling. As before, to avoid repetition, I have simply cross-referenced where necessary.

- **Constipation** See pages 112 and 119. But remember also that constipation can cause "overflow poo"—that is, more liquid or smaller poo that manages to escape past the large blockage. There is often a lack of control of this overflow poo. The solution here is not to try to get the child to control it but to eliminate it by removing the constipation.

- **Diarrhea** is often a symptom of constipation, although this might seem unlikely. It can be another form of overflow poo, when the blockage is so severe that only liquid poo (diarrhea) can get past it.

  Diarrhea can also be a symptom of an unbalanced microbiome—the body's balance of bacteria, or gut flora. Our bodies need what are often termed "good bacteria" to be healthy; however, these are frequently damaged.

The main culprits here are antibiotics, which are great at killing unwanted, or "bad," bacteria, but they unfortunately kill off the much-needed good bacteria too. Illness can also deplete the gut flora. In terms of the microbiome establishing itself at birth, there are two common practices that can inhibit the growth of good bacteria colonization. These are birth by cesarean section and formula feeding.[2] When babies are born vaginally they are coated in vaginal secretions from the mother, which help to establish the gut flora, whereas with a cesarean, the sterile birth environment prevents this colonization. Further, most mothers are also given antibiotics to prevent infection, and in some countries babies are given antibiotic eye drops immediately after birth, regardless of the mode of delivery. As far as feeding is concerned, breast milk contains the mother's good bacteria, which are transferred to the baby, whereas formula milk is not sterile, and the bacteria that it contains are "bad" rather than "good" (which is why it needs to be made up with boiling water). A formula-fed baby, therefore, does not get the same microbiome colonization as a breast-fed one.

If your child was born via cesarean, was formula-fed, or has had antibiotics at any point, a course of probiotics can help their gut flora to become healthy, which may have a positive impact on diarrhea and soiling.[3] Also try to include as much prebiotic food as possible in their diets to help to support the growth of good bacteria. Foods that contain prebiotics include garlic, onions, tomatoes, berries, bananas, flaxseed, and whole grains.

There are a few other physiological conditions that can cause diarrhea, and you should always consult a medical doctor for this reason. By far the most common cause is celiac disease, an autoimmune disorder in which the body reacts to gluten in food. In children the onset is usually between six months and two years, although it can happen much later. This extreme response from the immune system to the presence of gluten causes the body to effectively attack itself. The attack occurs in the small intestine, where damage is done to the villi—small fingerlike projections that coat the inside of the intestine and aid in the absorption of nutrients. In undiagnosed or untreated celiac disease, the damage to the villi is so severe that absorption of nutrients is dramatically affected. Common symptoms in children include slow weight gain, often known as "failure to thrive," diarrhea, abdominal distention (bloated tummy), and lack of energy. Celiac disease is fairly common, affecting one in every one hundred children; many cases remain undiagnosed, however, which means many are living with it unaware.

Finding the underlying cause of diarrhea should be the first-line approach; there is always a reason for it, and only when this is found can you reasonably expect the soiling to stop.

- **Potty and toilet refusal** Soiling is naturally linked to potty and toilet refusal. The suggested tips to resolve refusal therefore also apply to soiling—see page 102.

- **Anxiety** When we are anxious, our bodies enter what's known as "fight-or-flight" mode. Controlled by our sympathetic nervous system and caused by the secretion of cortisol (the stress hormone), this physiological effect happens automatically in response to perceived danger. In essence, it readies our bodies to either fight or run away from danger. In order for this to happen, blood needs to divert to the brain and the circulatory system and muscles, taking it away from other areas less involved in our immediate survival, including the digestive system. Importantly, when it comes to soiling, the fight-or-flight response also has an effect on the body's sphincters. This makes sense from an evolutionary perspective—to run quickly we need to empty waste from our bodies and make ourselves lighter. Hence soiling (or wetting) can take place as a response to fear and extreme anxiety.

  Children who are severely stressed and anxious may therefore soil because of a biological response to fear— one that is totally out of their conscious control. Causes of fear and anxiety are obviously individual, but common ones may include being in new situations (for instance, starting school or moving), the arrival of a new sibling and the associated fear of losing parental love, or living in a home where the parents often argue.

> Foster an environment of calm, compassion, and unconditional acceptance.

Shouting at or punishing the child for soiling only makes the problem worse. The solution is to identify and remove the cause of their fear or anxiety as much as possible and to foster an environment of calm, compassion, and unconditional acceptance.

Accidents can place an enormous strain on both parents and children alike. There are three key points to take away from this chapter. First, you must find the cause of the problem. Children do not intentionally choose to wet or soil themselves; there is always an underlying physical or emotional issue. Second, constipation is perhaps the top cause of all accidents, whether pee or poo, yet it is grossly overlooked. And third, accidents are nobody's fault, least of all your child's. The key is to stay calm and compassionate while, most important, working as a team—with your child and everyone who is involved in their care. This teamwork, along with some judicious detective work, is always the answer to surviving and, ultimately, resolving any toilet-training-related problems.

CHAPTER 7

Questions from Parents

Whenever I pick up a book like this, I always love to read stories from real parents, as I think they help to bring the advice to life. I have therefore included some of the questions I have been asked by parents concerning their children's toilet training, along with my answers, and I am extremely grateful to them for allowing me to do so. I have divided the questions into four sections: potty-training readiness, daytime toileting, night training, and poo problems. I hope you enjoy reading them and that you can apply them to your own situation, even if they differ slightly in some respects.

Potty-training readiness

The following questions and answers all relate to the starting of potty training and choosing the right time to begin.

Q: My son is eighteen months old and we use a potty in the morning and at diaper changes, with success both for pees and poo. However, he still does three to four poos a day at random times. He will tell me he is doing one as he does it. My question is, how do I know when to try potty training properly? I can't see that starting when he still poos so much is a good idea.

A: It sounds to me that you are doing a form of early potty training known as elimination communication* that is encouraging him to use the potty, perhaps with some form of trigger from you, such as making a noise or a gesture, or that you are following his signs of needing to use the potty, or perhaps both. This is a good start toward proper potty training, but I don't think it really signals readiness. There is a big difference between cueing, or following a child's cues and putting them on the potty, or accidentally "catching" wees and poos, and the child

---

* Elimination communication is a process in which parents hold their baby over a potty for pees and poos, initially aiming to "catch" something and later introducing cues—normally a sound—that become associated through a process of conditioning (a bit like dog training) in order that the baby will produce when held over the potty. They are not toilet trained in the sense of having proper bladder or bowel control, but they can remain dry and out of diapers for all or some of the time.

independently becoming continent by following
their body's sensations and proactively going to
the toilet, or holding on until they reach it. It is the
latter that needs to happen when properly potty
training.

I would say that your son is still a little young at
the moment. Research shows us that potty training
before twenty months rarely goes well. If your son
was showing signs of knowing that he needs a poo
before doing it, as opposed to telling you when he is
already going, I would suggest that you could start in
a couple of months' time. As he is only telling you
once he is going, however, I would recommend
holding off a little, probably waiting until nearer to
his second birthday. It's great that you have made a
start by normalizing the potty and hopefully when it
is the right time biologically, potty training should be
fairly easy for you.

In terms of the frequent pooing, while this could
be normal, it could also be a sign of constipation or
microbiome issues—an imbalance of gut flora. If the
poo is more like diarrhea or rabbit droppings or is
ribbonlike, I would investigate the possibility of
constipation with your doctor. If there is any
underlying problem, then potty training, when you
do start, will be much harder, so it's better to rectify
any issues now.

Q: My daughter has just turned two and tells me when she has done a pee or a poo in her nappy. We have had a potty in the house for the last six months, but she hasn't shown any particular interest in it. Should I start potty training now?

A: I don't think now would be a good time to start. Your daughter is just about old enough from a physiological point of view, by which I mean that she should be able to control the muscles that work to produce pee and poo and, most important, to keep it in; and her bladder capacity is now at a point where she can hold pee for a significant period of time. But what she doesn't have yet, from the sounds of things, is emotional readiness and awareness. Telling you that she has done a pee or a poo is a good start, but you need her to be telling you when she needs to go. This awareness of needing a pee or a poo before they actually happen is vital for training, in order to be able to make it to the potty or toilet in time.

In terms of having a potty around the house, I would usually recommend that this comes out shortly before training starts, not several months ahead, but as you have already had one out for six months I would not worry too much about that. I'd avoid making a big deal out of it, though, until a couple of weeks before you decide to start potty training, which, from what you have written, I would suggest will happen at some point in the next six months.

Q: My son will be three next month. We parent in a very child-led way and are waiting for him to decide when to potty train. He isn't showing any particular signs and doesn't really have any interest in the potty, so I'm not sure whether we should wait until he does. My concern is that I'm not sure he will ever tell us that he wants to start, but I don't want to push him if he's not ready.

A: I think you have hit the nail on the head when you say you're not sure that he will ever tell you that he wants to begin. There is a universal myth that all children will suddenly decide when they are ready to train and either do it totally by themselves or tell their parents that they want to start.

At almost three years old, your son is old enough from a biological perspective. By this I mean it is likely that the relevant muscles have developed enough for him to control both his bladder and bowels. His bladder can now hold much more fluid than it could eighteen months ago, and the hormonal regulation of urine production is probably now fairly well established. From an emotional point of view, your son is probably ready if he has fairly good communication skills—not necessarily just verbal, but gestures or signing too—and also follows simple instructions from you. The cherry on the top, in terms of readiness, would be his telling you that he needs to go to the toilet, or hiding, particularly when having a poo.

From what you have said, I would begin as soon as possible. Although you are making the decision to start, this doesn't mean that the whole process won't be child-led. In fact, the opposite is true. With gentle potty training, your son is very much in control, as far as possible, and the two of you will be working as a team, which sounds like a match for your parenting style.

Q: My son is two years and two months old, and for the last few weeks, he has started to potty train himself. He'll happily use the potty or the toilet both at home and when we are out. I'm expecting my second baby in a few weeks, and I wasn't intending to even begin some gentle pottying until after the baby and after Christmas, when he would be two and a half.

My question is, what should I do? Continue at his pace or encourage him to go more often and get him using pants rather than diapers? I'm aware that people say potty training can regress with a new arrival anyway, so I want to make everything as easy as possible for him.

A: What a fortunate and also difficult situation you are in! I would say that your son is definitely ready to start potty training, and I would strongly suggest that you follow his lead and embrace it. It sounds like now is definitely the time, and, as he is so keen, the chances are that it will be a straightforward process.

His timing when it comes to the new baby arriving isn't great from your perspective, though. Unfortunately, parenting isn't convenient, and things rarely work out as you plan. Sometimes it's about grabbing the opportunities as they arrive and trying to fit them into our complicated lives. There is a chance that he will regress when the new baby comes along, but there is just as much chance that he won't. Perhaps you may be finishing up potty training with a newborn in arms or, on the other hand, your son may be reliably dry by then. Certainly it would be nice to have only one child in diapers, from both financial and practical perspectives.

While there is never a perfect time, there is a time that's right for the individual child and their needs. In your position I would go for it now, starting off with a couple of days bare-bottomed at home, then moving to underwear only for a couple of days, before moving on to full clothing, hopefully before the baby arrives. Good luck!

Daytime toileting

The following questions all relate to daytime potty training, specifically pees on the potty or toilet and related accidents and concerns.

Q: I am really struggling with getting my toddler (she is two years and eight months old) to let me know when she needs a pee. For the last three or four months she has told me when she needs to poo or does it when we sit her on the toilet first thing in the morning. We had an attempt at potty training a couple of months ago, but she never really asked to go and had lots of accidents. After three weeks we stopped and went back to diapers. Then three weeks ago she kept asking to wear underwear. So we went for it and she is still having one or two accidents a day and mainly going for a pee when I persuade her to sit on the potty by bribing her. I am guessing you will say she isn't ready, but she refuses to let me put a nappy on her now, and three days after we started she would not put one on at bedtime and we have had nearly three weeks of dry naps and nights.

I cannot tell if she is not taking herself to the potty or telling me she needs to pee because she doesn't recognize the feeling, because she is too engrossed in her activity, or if it has become a testing behavior. She used to be better if naked, and at home she would occasionally take herself, but that also seems to have stopped. I really do not know how to help her. She doesn't really like pulling her underwear and trousers up and down, which I think would help because she seems happy when I leave her to go to the toilet by herself.

A: Contrary to your expectation, I actually do think your daughter is ready. There are a number of issues at play here. First, I think you need to be more involved initially and not expect your daughter to take herself to the toilet. By this I mean you should be helping her to recognize when she needs to go. I would do this by suggesting she comes with you to the toilet every time you go, by asking her on an hourly basis if she thinks she should go, and by watching for any nonverbal cues she shows shortly before a wee—this is especially important if she is engrossed in play, which is when it's common for accidents to occur.

Next, the bribing and rewards need to stop; they don't help her to learn to listen to her body; they just teach her to produce to get a treat. You need the former to happen, and it may actually be undermined by bribing her.

When you do begin training again, which I would do as soon as possible, it is important that you dispense with diapers in the daytime for good. The inconsistency of switching between underwear and diapers is confusing; your daughter needs to know that this is how it will be from now on—diapers only come out at night and that's it. This may mean some challenging days or weeks initially, but it is by far the best way to get through toilet training with the fewest accidents possible in the long term.

I would also suggest that you lose the underpants and clothes at first. As well as learning to use your potty, your daughter is having to contend with dressing and undressing, and this is too much at once. Spend the first two days with her totally bare-bottomed, before progressing to underwear and a top only for a couple of days. Only dress her fully toward the end of the first week, ensuring that clothes are potty-training-friendly—she shouldn't need your help to take down trousers, tights, or leggings or to lift up skirts, as this will reduce the chances of successful and stress-free potty training.

Last, I do wonder if there is a little bit of relationship work that needs to happen too. There seems to be a bit of a power struggle between you and your daughter. For potty training to be as successful and calm as possible, you need to be working on the same team. If the child is lacking control in other areas of their life, they will often fight to retain it when it comes to toileting. I think spending some time enjoying each other's company and rebonding would be time very well spent.

Q: We had good success with our nearly three-year-old, and she was using the potty quite happily. But she then went backward, and now it's 50/50 whether she uses her potty or demands a diaper. If we try to encourage her to use the potty she gets very upset, so we let her wear a diaper. She goes more happily at nursery, but rarely a poo. We have a fifteen-month-old who has started walking, and that may be a reason, so we're trying to make sure we connect with and support our eldest at the same time.

A: Regressions happen for a number of reasons. I think your primary goal needs to be looking for any triggers for your daughter's behavior. The fact that her sibling has just started walking could well be one, but there could be others. Look for anything causing her anxiety or fear in particular. You mention she goes to day care—I would be investigating this for starters. I would also check for any physiological causes; the two main elements to rule out are UTIs and constipation. If she has been affected by either of these, either currently or in the past, that could be the culprit. Even if she no longer has them, there could be residual fear of discomfort or pain. The same is true of your response to your daughter when she has accidents and doesn't make it to the potty on time.

I would suggest that you drop the diapers immediately in the daytime. You may well have a tricky couple of days with accidents and upset from your daughter, but you are sending mixed messages by still allowing her to have a diaper at times. She needs to understand that diapers are for night only. You may want to go right back to the beginning of potty training, spending a couple of quiet days at home with her bare-bottomed before moving on to underwear, with as much protection as possible in case of accidents. Try to take the pressure off, but keep the diapers away. Consistent messages are key.

Q: My little boy (eighteen months) started letting us know that he had been to, or needed, the toilet a few months ago. So, following his lead, we introduced a potty and have had good success so far. He does every poo in the toilet or potty and a lot of pees. I was leaving him diaper-free in the house and he was doing so well that I was looking at getting reusable training pants. Then we went on vacation for a week. During the day he was wet a lot of the time and peed without thinking, it seemed. However, during the night, he was totally dry, which was new. Since we've been home he appears to have regressed and is now wet again during the night and seems to actively pee on the floor during his nappy-free time. Is this a typical age or stage for regression or do you think the holiday has affected him? I'm trying to be child-led, but it's all starting to feel a bit forced. I feel as though he isn't ready, but he was doing so well for so long.

A: It sounds as if your son wasn't quite ready to potty train in the first place. Eighteen months is very young from both a physiological and an emotional point of view. It doesn't surprise me that days in the house and being nappy-free resulted in lots of potty usage, but time out of the house, dressed, especially in a different location, has resulted in an apparent regression. The aim with potty training is that children should be able to cope when clothed and not at home fairly soon after starting. Only when this happens do they really have true continence.

In your case, I think I would hold fire for another month or two, until your son indicates that he wants to use the potty again. Ordinarily, I would absolutely not advocate putting a child back in diapers, but as you started when he was most likely not properly ready I think this is your best bet right now. Ideally, you will be waiting for him to indicate emotional readiness—things like communicating when he needs to go to the toilet, taking himself to the potty (not just taking off his diaper), or hiding when he does a poo.

When you do restart it is important that he doesn't stay bare-bottomed for too long, as this can cause problems when putting him back into clothes, as you have found. I advocate only the first couple of days, after which I would put him into regular underwear (not training pants) for another couple of days before moving on to clothes by the end of the week. The only proviso here is to make sure that the clothes are potty-training-friendly; i.e., elasticated waists and things that are easy for him to take down and pull up without your help. It is only when children are unable to undress, go to the toilet, and redress that they are properly potty trained in my opinion. Similarly, true potty training requires the child to recognize their body signals and take themselves to the potty unprompted, and I'm not sure if this has happened so far in your case.

Potty training doesn't need to feel forced. If your child is physiologically and emotionally ready and you stay calm and consistent, working as a team, it can be incredibly gentle and compassionate. If things have felt forced to you, then I would suggest that this, once again, is an indication that it was just a little too early.

Q: We started a lazy kind of elimination communication (EC) at three months because we started noticing our baby's signs and it saved on washing pooey diapers! She seemed to genuinely prefer to use the potty, so whenever we were outside or in the bathroom we'd have diaper-off time and encourage the use of the potty with oodles of praise. I went back to work when she was almost one, so EC became a part-time affair. At age two we tried to go diaper-free during the day, as she was dry at home. The first few days, she was completely dry, even at day care, but more and more wet accidents seemed to happen, so the nursery asked us to revert back. When she was three we tried again. She refused to wear diapers, even when baby number two arrived.

Fast-forward to now, she's a bright, willful toddler who holds her pees until the last moment, then doesn't get to the toilet or potty on time. It's not just that she's distracted—she refuses to go when we suggest, shivering, going red, crossing her legs, that sort of thing. It's become a power struggle, I think. We've tried treating her for constipation (this helped for a bit), checking for infections at the doctor's, sticker charts, praise, being really relaxed about it, and ignoring the accidents. Some days, she will take herself and there are no accidents; other days, she urinates almost all the time, even just after she's been. We are at our wits' end and feel so guilty for pushing her too early and for when we lose our temper. (I really try not to, but it's so frustrating.) Help!

A: I do think there is a bit of a control issue going on here—not necessarily a power struggle, but I believe your daughter is probably sick of the whole potty-training thing. And I don't blame her; it's been an issue in your lives for so long. I think you need to make it less of a big deal and get back to teamwork.

First, I would lose the praise and stickers. These only work for the wrong reason. They don't teach your daughter to notice her body's signals, and they don't motivate her to use the potty or toilet because she wants to; there is a very real chance that they can delay true continence because of this. I think your priority should be to rebuild your daughter's trust surrounding toileting—and your trust in her. I suspect that nursery and a new baby arriving have both had a negative influence too. My main focus would be on removing the stress and anxiety surrounding toileting. If your daughter is in a state of high anxiety, and it sounds like she may be, then she will find it much harder to control her bladder. This can develop into a horrible cycle in which she is wetting, making both you and her upset, which causes more anxiety, then more wetting. Focus on lots of one-on-one time with her, without the constant pressure of toilet training. Invite her along to use the toilet with you whenever you go (which I would do hourly). Make sure that she can dress and undress herself and take her on a special shopping trip to get some underwear she loves, spending the day really trying to empathize with her.

That said, however, I suspect there is still an underlying physiological issue at work. It's interesting that she has previously been treated for constipation. I actually think it's still an issue, either because she is still chronically constipated and the treatment merely palliated things for a bit without solving the underlying problem and now it has come back (which is quite common) or because of fear surrounding the pain of constipation. I would take her to the doctor and ask for a referral to a pediatric gastroenterologist as soon as possible.

Q: My son is three years and three months old. While we are at home he doesn't wear pants or a diaper and uses the toilet independently. He usually wears a diaper or training pants when out and about, but he always wets them. We have tried pants, but he wets them too and doesn't tell me. What am I doing wrong? Do I just need to get rid of diapers and stick to pants, regardless of accidents? He is not dry at night yet either. I have always followed his lead, but there has been no improvement.

A: It does sound as if your son is capable of being diaperless in the daytime. I think the issue you have is the inconsistency between using diapers, underwear, and diaper-free time. When you are potty training it is really important to take a consistent approach so there are no mixed messages for the child to pick up on. This means the diapers need to go, at least in the daytime, anyway. Next, I would try to rein in the bare-bottomed time. This is great at home, but the child quickly becomes used to going to the toilet half naked, which understandably causes issues when they are clothed and away from home.

I would spend a few days—up to a week maximum—with just underwear and a top on at home. Use regular underwear and be prepared for accidents and lots of cleaning up. When he has the hang of things and the accidents become less frequent, add some trousers. Make sure that they are easy for him to pull up and down independently, so elasticated waists only. When you have spent a couple of days at home fully dressed, then you are ready to venture out of the house, remembering underwear only—no diapers or training pants.

In terms of the nights, I wouldn't expect this to happen for another six to twelve months. Day dryness usually precedes night dryness by quite a few months. It is common too for accidents to happen at night quite regularly in children under six or seven years of age. I wouldn't rush the night training yet; sort the daytime first, and the nights will follow.

Q: My daughter is five and in her first year at school. She potty trained fully just before her third birthday and we have had minimal accidents since then. Since she has been at school during the day, however, she has had several wetting accidents while there. She is obviously embarrassed, and I'm heartbroken for her. What should I do?

A: I can understand why you're so upset for your daughter. Wetting at this age, and especially at school, is actually really common, though. I suspect if you speak to her teachers, they will reassure you that she isn't the only one going through this.

There are a number of reasons why wetting is more likely to happen at school than at home, and it would be worth checking that none of these applies to your daughter.

First, some schools do restrict bathroom breaks. This is clearly not in the children's best interests, particularly those as young as your daughter. The presumption is that children should be able to wait for an hour or two between breaks before needing to go to the toilet, and while this may be true physiologically, it takes no account of the child's psychological development. So while you may plan to go to the toilet during a break just in case you need to go later, this is not something that children do. Similarly, your daughter may be distracted by play or work and may not realize she needs the toilet until it is almost too late. At this point, if the teacher prohibits her from going, an accident is inevitable. I would have a chat with a teacher to make sure she is allowed free access to the bathroom whenever she needs it, regardless of whether it's in the middle of a lesson.

Next, check whether she struggles with her clothing. Starting school often means far more restrictive clothes, which can really slow down going to the toilet. If your daughter is wearing school trousers or tights, she may struggle to remove these quickly enough independently. Simply swapping to elasticated waistbands and socks could help here.

Last, I would check how your daughter is coping with school in general. If she is feeling anxious or stressed, then this is likely to increase the chances of her having a wetting accident. Ensuring that she is as calm and settled as possible at school, both academically and from a friendship point of view, is really important.

Q: This may seem like a silly question, but my son is four and has been potty trained for some time. When we are out and about he comes into the ladies' toilets with me when he needs to go to the toilet. I don't feel comfortable with him going into the men's without me. At what age should he be going in there alone?

A: I think you are absolutely doing the right thing. There is no set age when boys should be made to go into the men's toilets. If he or you are uncomfortable with it, then keep doing what you are doing. Your son can still stand to pee, by lifting the toilet seat in the ladies' room, if he prefers. (I actually much prefer the idea of unisex toilets for this reason.) My own sons tended to venture into the men's toilets without me when they were around nine or ten years old, although they would still choose to go into a stall, rather than stand at the urinals with somebody they have never met before—something I can totally understand.

Night training

The following questions and answers focus on the issue of nighttime toilet training—namely, when to begin and how to cope with accidents.

Q: My son is almost three years old and is completely dry during the day. At night, we put him on the toilet to pee at 10 p.m. and again, in the middle of the night, at 3 or 4 a.m. This hasn't been too hard, as I'm waking up for night feeds anyway (my youngest is ten months), but if we miss the night waking, it often results in a wet bed. My baby is sleeping for longer stretches now, and my toddler is very upset by wet pajamas in the morning. He is adamant that he won't wear a diaper or pull-up. Is it simply a case of riding it out, or is there something else I can do?

A: Your son is pretty young to be dry at night. It also doesn't sound as if he is ready. Your lifting twice a night is effectively preventing him from wetting the bed, but it is not teaching him anything. He isn't learning to control his bladder at night because of this and is unlikely to do so while it continues.

If you are happy to keep doing what you are doing, then you don't have an issue because in time, as his body matures, he will develop continence. But your lifting is going to have to keep going until it does. If, on the other hand, your baby is sleeping and you don't want to get up twice a night to take your son to the toilet, then you will need to find a compromise until he is ready to night train. This may be using some form of cloth training pants that look and feel less like diapers but provide more protection. Cloth diapers can also work well, as the child feels some of the wetness, but they don't look or feel like regular diapers.

On average, children usually attain night continence around ten months after reliable daytime dryness; you don't say when your son was potty trained in the daytime, but from what you have written I am going to make a guess that you have around three to six months to go until you start to see proper night continence. The question is, how long do you want to continue with getting up and taking him to the toilet? And the answer to that will be the best guide as to what to do right now.

Q: I was wondering if you can give me any advice on night training my four-year-old daughter. She has been dry in the daytime since she was two and a half years old, which was her decision and she did it all herself at her own pace. She has recently commented that she doesn't want to wear a diaper at bedtime, but nothing more has been said or done. Her diaper is full in the morning, and she loves her milk too much at bedtime to give that up. She has recently started school, so I didn't want to add more pressure to this recent big change in her life.

A: Most of the signs are pointing to your daughter being ready now. As she is four years old and has been dry in the daytime for the last year and a half I would suggest that she is physiologically able to go through the night without a diaper. Her desire to not wear one at night highlights that she is emotionally ready to begin too, despite having recently started school. The only sticking point is the full diaper in the morning. This may not actually be an issue, however, as it could be that she is filling it close to the morning as she begins to stir, or even when she just wakes. Often, if a diaper is on at these times, children will use it. I don't think you need to give up the bedtime milk; a normal amount really should not be an issue.

The place to start is a chat with your daughter. Tell her that you think she could get through the night without a diaper now and that you understand that she would prefer to lose it too. Explain to her that she needs to go to the toilet immediately before bed and as soon as she wakes up in the morning—and if she wakes in the night she should call for you to come and take her to the toilet if she is not confident going alone. You should also have a chat about how it's normal to have accidents when you are still learning and that it's okay if she wets the bed now and again, explaining that you did as well when you were her age.

Because bedwetting is common when children first toilet train—and normal for a good few months or years afterward too—being prepared is key. Get a good mattress protector, and consider using the large disposable bed mats that you can buy in most supermarkets. If she doesn't already have a night-light, put one in her room so that if you don't hear her call and she doesn't want to take herself to the bathroom, she can come to you when she needs to go.

Finally, share in her achievements with her, but go easy on the praise. Praising continence too much can really backfire, especially when children go through temporary regressions. Instead, focus on showing her that you have noticed what she has been doing and ask her if she feels proud of herself when she makes it through the night with no wetting.

Q: My son is four years and two months old. He has been using the potty and toilet in the day for more than a year now with no accidents since he started. However, he still wears pull-ups in bed and will

wake up with them full. Any suggestions as to how
to get him out of diapers at night?

A: It sounds like your son is ready to lose the overnight
diapers. The fact he has been dry in the day for more
than a year tells me that he probably can get through
the night without them. The question is, does he
want to?

While he has a diaper at night I think he's going
to continue using it; there is no reason for him to get
up and go to the toilet. Some children also fill their
diaper first thing in the morning if the parents don't
get to them immediately when they wake up. This
isn't an indication that they are unable to get through
the night without a diaper—just that they need to go
to the potty or toilet as soon as they wake.

I would start with having a chat with your son.
Tell him you believe he is ready and ask how he feels
about leaving the diapers off. I would suggest reading
a book to him or watching a DVD together about
nighttime toilet training to really prepare him. Agree
on a night to begin. If he is at school or you work, I
would suggest a Friday night. Make sure he has a
good night-light in his room and can see his potty, or
that he can get to the toilet easily without having to
open doors or turn on lights; also, let him know he

can call for you in the night if he needs to go to the toilet. Get a good mattress protector, and consider making the bed up with two or three layers of sheets and a disposable bed mat in between each, so that if accidents occur you can quickly take off the wet layer, leaving a new dry one without all the fuss of putting on clean sheets in the night. If he has an accident, empathize with him; tell him it's okay because he's still learning and you trust he will do it soon. Most important of all, though, stay calm and don't go back to the diapers once you have started.

Q: My twenty-month-old is pretty good during the day, with the odd slip-up where she forgets to tell us "potty time" until she's done it. Overnight, we're getting three out of seven dry nights (only once has she woken in the middle of the night to say "potty time"). She's still in a nighttime diaper. Is there a way of getting her out of diapers without risking wet beds, or do we just wait? We already take her directly to the potty whenever she wakes after five o'clock in the morning.

A: I would work on the daytime potty training first. Your daughter is very young to be dry at night. Most children attain night continence six to twelve months after they have been reliably dry in the daytime. As your daughter is still having the odd accident in the day I would hold on until she is reliably dry in the day, then wait another couple of months before losing the diapers at night. Most children can differentiate between wearing underwear in the day and diapers at night—in other words, the night diapers don't cause a problem with daytime continence. In your situation, waiting really is the best option and certainly the least stressful one for the whole family.

Q: My little boy is six years old and still regularly wets the bed, maybe once a week. He was potty trained when he was two years and nine months old and everything went fine. He was out of diapers at night just before his fourth birthday, but we have had fairly regular accidents ever since that seem to show no sign of stopping. Should I be worried?

A: At this age, a quarter of boys still wet the bed occasionally. Once a week would certainly fit into my definition of "occasionally." If either you or your partner has a history of bed-wetting in childhood yourselves, then your son's risk is even higher. Most children outgrow bed-wetting as they get older and their bodies mature. If your son is still wetting in a year's time, you could ask your family doctor for a referral to a pediatric urologist. (It is quite likely that you won't be able to get a referral before your son is seven.) Treatment of nocturnal enuresis (bed-wetting) may include using a special alarm, medication that helps to control the production of urine at night, and sometimes behavioral therapy. I would also look into the possibility of constipation, which is a common and often a missed cause of night wetting.

Most important, stay calm and compassionate when your son has an accident, reminding yourself he is not doing it on purpose—he can't help it. As angry or frustrated as you may feel, he is likely to be as sad and embarrassed. Get a good mattress protector, and let him know that it's okay to have accidents. If you remember any experiences from your own childhood, discuss how you felt with him. Keeping stress to a minimum is important for the whole family.

Poo problems

The following questions are all about problems with poo, both in the day and at night.

Q: What's the best way to tackle poo withholding? Our son potty trained very easily, without incident, but won't poo anywhere other than at home. So if we have a busy few days where we're not at home much, he may not go at all. I'm worried this isn't healthy.

A: This is a tricky one, as I don't think the issue is withholding so much as your son being uncomfortable pooing in an unfamiliar place. This is actually quite common, affecting individuals all the way through to adulthood. Many adults will find it hard to poo on vacation, for instance. The next thought that comes to mind is that your son may have an issue with public toilets and a lack of privacy— again, something many people struggle with right into adulthood. I also wonder if he doesn't like to use toilets other than your own at home for a specific reason—for instance, the absence of a step or handrails. We actually need to have our feet flat on the floor (or a step) in order to be able to poo effectively. If your son is sitting with his feet dangling on a toilet when you are out, he may find it physically difficult to poo. The answer here, therefore, is to take a portable step or potty out with you. The familiarity of these objects alone may help, but being able to poo while in a semi-squatting position is key.

Q: My son decided at two years and three months old to stop wearing diapers and went dry pretty much straightaway, day and night. However, more than a year later, at three years and six months, he's still doing poos in his pants. We've had some success getting poos in the potty and toilet; when he does it we make a big fuss and give lots of positive praise and we treat poos in pants as non-events, simply taking him to the toilet to clean him up and asking where the poo belongs, to which he always replies "the toilet." He knows where he should be doing them, but he just has no interest in doing so. Repeatedly, he tells me he'll do them in the toilet when he's tall like daddy! We've been patient, but it would be great if you have any words of wisdom or ideas to help us move things along.

A: I think the first thing I would like you to stop is the praise when your son poos in the toilet or potty; this doesn't actually help him to feel confident doing so and may actually reduce the chance that it will happen again. I would focus instead on telling him what he has done and letting him know you have noticed—"That's a big poo you did in the potty, isn't it?" If he ever shows signs that he has tried to get to the potty but accidentally poos in his pants, then it is far more important to recognize this than successful poos on the potty. Here I would say, "Gosh, I saw you trying to get to the potty—you tried so hard to get there. You will manage it soon; it just takes time to learn." This trying should definitely not be treated as a non-event. Any time he tries is important, whether he succeeds or not.

There are two main points I would focus on in terms of getting the poo in the potty or toilet: privacy and squatting. First, by pooing in his pants, your son may be able to escape to another room, or hide, so that nobody watches him poo—this is privacy he probably doesn't get if he's on the potty or toilet. Make sure you give him as much privacy as possible then—for instance, putting the potty behind your sofa or pulling your bathroom door closed. I would also get a special step that can help him to sit in a squatting position on the toilet, holding his legs slightly higher than his waist. This physiologically optimal position can help him to poo but is not one he can get into without the step.

I wonder also if you have tried looking at children's books about poo and why we poo on the toilet, plus where the poo goes once it is flushed away. If you haven't, then reading these together would be a good idea. Last, I would make sure that your son is always able to see you poo on the toilet; as unpleasant as it sounds, this really normalizes the whole process for him and he is more likely to imitate you.

Q: My son is sixteen months old. He is looked after by a
nanny two days a week and the rest of the time by
me or family. He is a very happy and calm kid. In the
first year I used to be able to tell if he was going to
have a pee. Nowadays I can't, as he seems rather busy
with toddling. He also struggles a bit with pooing (he
pushes hard), but he likes to do it standing up and
concentrating on playing with something. He is at
the moment hating diaper changes (didn't use to
complain). I wonder what the transition to potty will
be like—to start with transitioning from standing to
sitting.

A: Your son is very young at the moment. I wouldn't
take the dislike of diaper changing as a sign that he is
ready to potty train. I suspect you have around six
months or so until daytime training. I would want
him to be at least twenty months old, to have fairly
good communication skills, and to either be able to
tell you when he is about to have a pee or a poo or
possibly go and hide when he poos.

Standing and concentrating on a toy while pooing
is very normal. The toy helps him to relax, by taking
his mind off things a little. A good toy to use is
bubble mixture; encouraging him to blow bubbles

will help him to relax his anal sphincter and the muscles around his rectum, allowing the poo to come out more easily. In terms of the standing, we really need to have our feet flat on the floor when we poo, which is why toddlers find it difficult to poo when sitting on a toilet with their legs dangling unsupported. Squatting is the ideal pooing position, though; you can actually get special squat stools for children to use while they poo on the toilet, which is something to bear in mind for when you do begin training. I suspect he will find this position more comfortable than standing, which means the transition will happen naturally.

What I would like to pick up on, though, is that your son finds it difficult to poo. I would be mindful of constipation, which has a very negative effect on toilet training. I would spend some time rectifying this now, so that it doesn't become a problem in the future. Make sure that he is taking in lots of fluids and plenty of fiber-rich food. If things don't improve, then I would consider any potential allergies and intolerances and possibly a visit to the doctor, as some constipation does need medical treatment. The great thing is that you are aware of all this before training starts, which means the whole journey is much more likely to be a positive and easy one for you all.

Q: When should you expect children to be able to wipe their own bottoms after having a poo? My son is five, and if he is left to do so independently he doesn't do a very good job!

A: I think your son is around the age when I would expect completely independent bottom wiping; however, I wouldn't expect him to do a particularly good job of it for a few more years. There are a few things that you can do that may help a little until then. First, make sure you teach him. This means encouraging him to look at the toilet paper and only stopping wiping when it is clean. Next, you may consider getting some moist toilet wipes—these can be a little more effective at cleaning and slightly easier for children to use. Last, make sure you don't ever hurry him up when he is wiping; encourage him to take as much time as he needs to finish. Rushing undoubtedly means they don't do a very good job!

I hope that you can see from these questions and my answers that there is no one-size-fits-all when it comes to potty training. The experience is different for every single family and every child within that family. Each child will do things at different times—some earlier, some later, and some dead on average. While there are many shared difficulties, the solutions are not necessarily the same, although you will have seen that some common themes underpin most issues.

Keeping the idea of individuality in mind is important; don't ever be tempted to judge your child against another— or yourself against another parent. Each and every one of you is on your own unique journey.

A Closing Note

If you found this book before embarking on the potty-training journey, I hope that you are now more confident about the process—from when to start to what preparation you need to do and how to actually get going. I also hope that you feel equipped to tackle any obstacles that may crop up along the way. Remember, accidents are normal and common; the keys to getting through them are knowledge, preparation, empathy, and working as a team with your child.

If you found this book after beginning potty training, perhaps because you were looking for help with tackling a certain issue, I hope that you now have more understanding of it and feel better prepared to deal with it. Once again, the keys are knowledge, preparation, empathy, and working as a team with your child. Your responses and reactions matter:

You need to stay calm and positive. If you have been struggling with potty-training issues for some time, it is understandably hard to remain calm and positive. I hope this book has helped a little with this, but you must also take some time to take care of your own emotional and physical needs. Don't push them aside. Your self-care really matters—it helps you, and it helps you to better help your child.

Having potty trained four children of my own, I know it can be challenging. I have coped with poo withholding, bed-wetting until a late age, constipation, early training, late training and toilet refusal. There is not much I haven't seen or dealt with. As a parenting coach, I've seen countless families get through this rite of passage as well, even when things got tricky and self-doubt creeped in. Quick fixes that sound too good to be true usually are, and competitive impulses to meet or beat another child's milestones are not the answer either; they'll only dial up your child's anxiety. Instead, you'll achieve success by working together with your child, with good helpings of compassion, empathy, and patience— or what I like to call gentle potty training.

Acknowledgments

I would like to say a huge thank-you to all the families who have allowed me to feature their questions in this book, and to those I have worked with over the last ten years for allowing me to share their potty-training journey. Thanks also to the team at TarcherPerigee for making this book a reality.

References

Chapter 1

1   "Appendix 8 Normal Urine Output": www.gosh.nhs
    .uk/file/869/download?token=SIiqGov5, accessed online,
    September 13, 2016.

2   Sillén, U., "Bladder Function in Healthy Neonates and Its
    Development during Infancy," *Journal of Urology*, 166, no. 6
    (December 2001): 2376–81.

3   Kamperis, K., et al., "The Circadian Rhythm of Urine
    Production, and Urinary Vasopressin and Prostaglandin E2
    Excretion in Healthy Children," *Journal of Urology* 171, no. 6,
    part 2 (June 2004): 2571–5.

4   Aikawa, T., Kasahara, T., and Uchiyama, M., "The
    Arginine-Vasopressin Secretion Profile of Children with
    Primary Nocturnal Enuresis," *European Urology* 33,
    supplement 3 (1998): 41–4.

5   Mirmiran, M., Maas, Y. G., and Ariagno, R. L., "Development of Fetal and Neonatal Sleep and Circadian Rhythms," *Sleep Medicine Review* 7, no. 4 (August 2003): 321–34.

6   Silva, M., Mallozi, M., and Ferrari, G., "Salivary Cortisol to Assess the Hypothalamic-Pituitary-Adrenal Axis in Healthy Children under 3 Years Old," *Jornal de Pediatria*, 83, no. 2, (March–April 2007): 121–6.

7   Kamperis, et al., "The Circadian Rhythm of Urine Production."

Chapter 2

1   Johns Hopkins Medicine: http://www.hopkinsmedicine .org/healthlibrary/conditions/pediatrics/toilet-training _90,P02300, accessed online, September 6, 2016.

2   Ibid.

3   Jansson, U., et al., "Voiding Pattern and Acquisition of Bladder Control from Birth to Age 6 Years—A Longitudinal Study," *Journal of Urology*, 174, no. 1: (July 2005): 289–93.

4   Largo, R., Gianciaruso, M., and Prader, A., "Development of Intestinal and Bladder Control from Birth until the 18th

Year of Age. Longitudinal Study," *Swiss Medical Weekly*, 108, no. 5 (February 4, 1978): 155–60.

5   Taubman, B., "Toilet Training and Toileting Refusal for Stool Only: A Prospective Study," *Pediatrics* 99, no. 1 (January 1997): 54–58.

6   Blum, N., Taubman, B., and Nemeth, N., "Relationship between Age at Initiation of Toilet Training and Duration of Training: A Prospective Study," *Pediatrics* 111, no. 4 (April 2003): 810–4.

7   Mota, D., and Barros, A., "Toilet Training: Methods, Parental Expectations and Associated Dysfunctions," *Journal de Pediatria* 84, no. 1 (January–February 2008): 9–17.

Chapter 3

1   FDA position statement on the safety and effectiveness of antibacterial soaps: http://www.fda.gov/NewsEvents/Newsroom/PressAnnouncements/ucm517478.htm, accessed online, September 23, 2016.

Chapter 4

1   de Jong, Y., et al., "Urinating Standing versus Sitting: Position Is of Influence in Men with Prostate Enlargement.

A Systematic Review and Meta-Analysis," *PLoS One* 9, no. 7 (July 2014): #c101320.

2   Warneken, F., and Tomasello, M., "Extrinsic Rewards Undermine Altruistic Tendencies in 20-Month-Olds," *Developmental Psychology* 44, no. 6 (November 2008): 1785–8.

3   Henderlong, J., and Lepper, M. R., "The Effects of Praise on Children's Intrinsic Motivation: A Review and Synthesis," *Psychological Bulletin* 128, no. 5 (September 2002): 774–95.

Chapter 5

1   Jansson, U., Hanson, M., Sillén, U. and Hellström, A., "Voiding Pattern and Acquisition of Bladder Control from Birth to Age 6 Years—a Longitudinal Study," *Journal of Urology* 174, no. 1 (July 2005): 289–93.

2   Largo, R., Gianciaruso, M. and Prader, A., "Development of Intestinal and Bladder Control from Birth until the 18th Year of Age. Longitudial Study," *Swiss Medical Weekly* 108, no. 5 (February 4, 1978): 155–60.

3   Mota, D., et al., "Longitudinal Study of Sphincter Control in a Cohort of Brazilian Children," *Jornal de Pediatria* 86, no. 5 (September–October 2010): 429–34.

REFERENCES

4 Butler, R., and Heron, J., "The Prevalence of Infrequent Bedwetting and Nocturnal Enuresis in Childhood: A Large British Cohort," *Scandinavian Journal of Urology and Nephrology* 42, no. 3 (2008): 257–64.

5 Muellner, S., "Development of Urinary Control in Children: Some Aspects of the Cause and Treatment of Primary Enuresis," *Journal of the American Medical Association* 172 (March 19, 1960): 1256–61.

6 van Dommelen, P., et al., "The Short- and Long-Term Effects of Simple Behavioral Interventions for Nocturnal Enuresis in Young Children: A Randomized Controlled Trial," *Journal of Pediatrics* 154, no. 5 (May 2009): 662–6.

7 Howe, A., and Walker, C., "Behavioral Management of Toilet Training, Enuresis, and Encopresis," *Pediatric Clinics of North America* 39, no. 3 (June 1992): 413–32.

8 Arnell, H., et al., "The Genetics of Primary Nocturnal Enuresis: Inheritance and Suggestion of a Second Major Gene on Chromosome 12q," *Journal of Medical Genetics* 34, no. 5 (May 1997): 360–5.

Chapter 6

1 Fry, C., Wu, C., and Mundy, A., "Bladder Instability and Detrusor Smooth Muscle Function," *Experimental Physiology*, 84(1) (January 1999), pp. 161–9.

2 Rutayisire, E., et al., "The Mode of Delivery Affects the Diversity and Colonization Pattern of the Gut Microbiota during the First Year of Infants' Life: A Systematic Review," *BMC Gastroenterology* 16, no. 1 (July 30, 2016): 86; Bentley, J., et al., "Gestational Age, Mode of Birth and Breastmilk Feeding All Influence Acute Early Childhood Gastroenteritis: A Record-Linkage Cohort Study," *BMC Pediatrics* 16 (April 27, 2016): 55.

3 Hashemi, A., Villa, C., and Comelli, E., "Probiotics in Early Life: A Preventative and Treatment Approach," *Food Functions* 7, no. 4 (April 2016): 1752–68.

Recommended Resources
and Further Reading

ONLINE

www.sarahockwell-smith.com

www.facebook.com/GentlePottyTrainingBook
The Gentle Potty Training Book on Facebook

www.i-c-c-s.org International Children's Continence
Society

Poo Goes Home to Pooland app—available in iTunes

POTTY-TRAINING BOOKS FOR CHILDREN

Have You Seen My Potty?, Mij Kelly, Hodder Children's
Books (2008)

Lulu's Loo, Camilla Reid, Bloomsbury Publishing
(2010)

On My Potty, Leslie Patricelli, Walker Books (2010)

Where's the Poop?, Julie Markes, HarperFestival (2004)

This Little Potty, Ladybird (2012)

POTTY-TRAINING BOOKS FOR CHILDREN, SPECIFICALLY ABOUT POO

It Hurts When I Poop!, Howard J. Bennett, Magination Press (2007)

Meet the Poo's, Rob Renée, Lulu.com (2013)

Everybody Poos, Taro Gomi, Frances Lincoln Children's Books (2004)

BOOKS FOR TRANSITIONING TO THE BIG TOILET FROM A POTTY

Captain of the Toilet, Rose Inserra, Barron's Educational Series (2013)

POTTY-TRAINING VIDEOS FOR CHILDREN

Elmo's Potty Time, Abbey Home Media Group (2009)

Bear in the Big Blue House: Potty Time with Bear, Walt Disney Studios (2005)

Potty Power: For Boys & Girls, Consumervision (2004)

Go Potty Go!: Potty Training for Tiny Toddlers, Wonderscape (2009)

RECOMMENDED PRODUCTS

Squatty Potty—toilet squatting step, www.squattypotty
.com

Potette Plus—folding portable potty, www.potette.com

BabyLegs—to keep legs warm during bare-bottomed
training, www.babylegs.com

Shewee—portable urination device for females to use when
traveling: www.shewee.com

TravelJohn—portable urinal for males to use when
traveling: www.traveljohn.com

Piddlepad—to protect car seats and strollers from accidents,
www.summerinfant.com

Index

About the Author

Sarah Ockwell-Smith is a trained prenatal teacher, birth and postnatal doula, pediatric homeopath, and the cofounder of GentleParenting.com. Her parenting blog at SarahOckwell-Smith.com is read by two million parents each year. She is the author of several other parenting guides, including *Gentle Discipline* and *BabyCalm*.

Sarah lives with her family, including four school-age children, along with cats and assorted farm animals, in a 350-year-old cottage in rural Essex, UK.

For more information, visit www.SarahOckwell-Smith.com.